a STILL & QUIET SOUL

a STILL & QUIET SOUL

embracing contentment

CATHY MESSECAR

LEAFWOOD
PUBLISHERS

A STILL AND QUIET SOUL
Embracing Contentment

Copyright 2011 by Cathy Messecar

ISBN 978-0-89112-283-8
LCCN 2010046400

Printed in the United States of America

LIBRARY OF CONGRESS CATALOGING-IN-PUBLICATION DATA
Messecar, Cathy.
A still and quiet soul : embracing contentment / by Cathy Messecar.
   p. cm
ISBN 978-0-89112-283-8
1. Contentment--Religious aspects--Christianity. I. Title.
BV4647.C7M47 2011
241'.4--dc22

        2010046400

Cover design by Thinkpen Design, Inc.
Interior text design by Sandy Armstrong

Leafwood Publishers
1626 Campus Court
Abilene, Texas 79601
1-877-816-4455 toll free

For current information about all Leafwood titles, visit our Web site:
www.leafwoodpublishers.com

11 12 13 14 15 16 / 7 6 5 4 3 2 1

DEDICATION

*I thank our heavenly Father for all his gifts and for so
perfectly shaping my husband David's heart to embrace mine.*

*And to our Father for completing both our hearts by
bringing Russell and Sheryle to us and through them Pam,
Natalie, and Molly, and Hito, Jack, Adam, and Jolie.*

CONTENTS

ACKNOWLEDGEMENTS

From my heart I give thanks for the bevy of friends who understand writers and provide shady spots in life, giving us the opportunity and time to write and the much-needed critiques. To the folks in my Life Group at my home church, who consistently support my writing and speaking, I remain grateful.

To Doris Allen, Pat Schuler, Jan Tickner, Sherry Rushing, Sheryle Bazan, Russell Stewart, thank you for the early read-throughs of this work. All of your helpful suggestions prodded me to dig deeper into the Word, pray more, and re-write often. A special thanks to Leslie Wilson for early editing. I always learn from you.

To five long-distance-friends, The Word Quilters—Trish Berg, Terra Hangen, Brenda Nixon, Karen Robbins, Leslie Wilson—your constant devotion to our group spreads hope in my heart. You prayed for me, and then you prayed some more.

To the men and women who contributed their personal testimonies, you enriched this work by giving readers a glimpse of your varied lives, your love for the Lord, your struggles, victories, and learning of contentment.

To the many people who supported me through private prayers, I have asked a special blessing for you and yours. To my newspaper column readers, you continually lift my spirits by letting me know when a column or a word I borrowed from the Lord helped you.

To the staff at Leafwood Publishers and Director, Dr. C. Leonard Allen, in particular, thank you for the opportunity to share my thoughts and work with you once again.

Dear Reader:

I'm keenly aware of those times when total contentment settles upon me, when nothing niggles at my conscience causing unrest. I include in this list the nights when my adult children and their children rest safe and sound in their homes. They abide in their nests, as my husband and I do in ours. Add a soft rainfall, evidence of God tending the earth, and my night becomes ideal. Those circumstances come as close to perfect as nights on this earth ever could. Contentment sweeps over me. A sweet sleep descends.

But what about opposite days when life-glitches hobble me? Sometimes, it seems the smallest negative happening can topple a glass of milk into my day, soaking the seams of morning, noon, and evening, dampening what I thought would be a beatitude day, a blessed day. On those days, what causes my thoughts to turn from blessed to beat down? Can I ignore the spilled milk and go about my day contented, extending goodwill to others?

God wrote the ultimate Contentment Manual, so this study guide, *A Still and Quiet Soul: Embracing Contentment*, serves only as a supplement. We'll consider how biblical characters faced their ordinary days, their disappointments, and their triumphs. You'll read first-person accounts of current believers and sidle up to their mishaps and successes to see anew how prayer, trust, and praise undergirds contentment.

Journey with me and let's discover what—or better yet—Who, nurtures contentment within each of us.

Cathy Messecar

Chapter One

A STILL AND QUIET SOUL

Contentment

But I have stilled and quieted my soul;
like a weaned child with its mother,
like a weaned child is my soul within me.

Psalm 131:2

The psalmist's reflections about quieting himself waltzed around in my heart for months. They slow-danced with questions about contentment, but the waltz faltered when I remembered the many difficulties in life. Soon, the waltz stopped completely, as I imagined contentment wrapping her arms around tragic events. How is it possible for contentment and tragedies to remain in rhythm?

Allow your mind to dwell on contentment for a week or so and questions will surface. I don't have all the answers, but I've experienced enough of life to know that learning contentment is worth the journey.

Consider the psalmist's portrayal of his quieted soul:

My heart is not proud, O LORD,
my eyes are not haughty;
I do not concern myself with great matters
or things too wonderful for me.
But I have stilled and quieted my soul;

like a weaned child with its mother,
like a weaned child is my soul within me.
O Israel, put your hope in the LORD
both now and forevermore.

Psalm 131

Question marks dot the margins in my Bible, including the space beside this psalm. When David wrote these words, he wrote from an obvious state of contentment. I compare my life and wonder how far concern over problems can roam without getting tangled in the barbs of discontent. Do some of the gifts from God, "the things too wonderful," deserve a simple thank you of acceptance, the gifts not to be over contemplated?

How can I be sure that my eyes are not haughty, that I have not become proud? When will I quit relying on tangibles such as money in the bank? How can I learn to better trust God? How can I reach the state of contentment that David possessed when he penned these words?

Meditation on this psalm led me to these thoughts.

Picture a helpless infant. He has loving parents plus two sets of doting grandparents, who cater to his normal needs about every three hours. In addition to those needs, he may even be colicky or fractious. This helpless infant can only cry out when he lacks nourishment or comfort, unable to do anything for himself. He cannot put food into his mouth, fasten on a clean diaper, or renew his mind to put a positive spin on a later than usual meal.

Fast forward a few years, the infant is now a preschooler, a "weaned child." He lives in a loving home and now resides in a pleasant place—in between helplessness and knowledge of the world's problems. He has learned to trust his parents. He knows that at lunch time his mother or daddy will offer a peanut butter sandwich. He also grasps beyond-needs-care because he has experienced their over-the-top love. He has even learned that his daddy or mother might give him a little cup of pudding as a treat.

He knows they will tuck soft covers around his shoulders at night. He trusts their cheery faces will be nearby when he awakens. The weaned child has learned to tone down his hollering, to quiet himself, because he trusts his parents to support him.

This psalm declares that adults who put their trust in the Lord "both now and forevermore" can learn and embrace contentment, no matter what obstacles they may face. The secret lies in co-habitation with God, much as a close-knit physical family lives together, because trust begins when we know reliable persons intimately.

The Journey to Contentment

A path back to childhood trust lays a foundation for contentment. By adulthood we have tasted the tree of knowledge of good and evil, but we can be steered back to the arms of God through Jesus and his Holy Spirit. A person can learn to hope in the Lord and quiet their soul like a weaned child with its mother. We can journey to contentment—no matter the outward circumstances—if we run backward to childlike trust.

My five-year-old grandson Jack watched news reports about approaching storms in the Gulf of Mexico. His family and ours live one hundred miles from the South Texas coast where moist air often collides with cooler air gliding down from the plains, causing dark clouds and greenish skies to appear overhead. Besides frequent thunderous weather, tropical storms make threats of projected landfall and some rumble ashore in late summer through fall. After hearing a weatherman's prediction of bad weather, Jack said, "I wish I was four again and didn't know about hurricanes."

Jack had barely stepped beyond the protective weaned stage, just beyond the Garden of Eden's threshold where thistles pushed up through the ground. Even though Jack remained under the protection of his parents, he began to understand the worries of the world—things he had no power to change.

Even though adults see and experience the evils of the world, we can journey back to childlike faith and trust in our Father because we have a gentle teacher and friend beside us. His name is Jesus. His energy lives within us to make us new, to mold us, and to change us to trust the Father as he does.

The Apostle Paul referenced this power in his letter to the Colossians. Paul desired to help others move toward a perfect life in Christ, including contentment. He said he could accomplish this task through Christ: "To this end I labor, struggling with all his energy, which so powerfully works in me" (1:29).

Adults journeying to contentment give their lives into the care of their loving Father, the good parent, who knows what is best for the grown-up Christian. Although we have tasted good and evil, we have also tasted the great comfort of our Heavenly Father. Our full-of-loving-kindness Father watches constantly over this world, and generously distributes powerful energy through Jesus Christ to those who rely on him as Savior and Lord.

Life's Average Report Card

Over my lifetime, I gradually began to understand that God's gift of peace isn't founded on the square footage of my home, the quality of the clothes in my closet, my love life, or paycheck. Blessings and glitches crowd every twenty-four-hour day, and I've seen that life mirrors an average report card. It doesn't contain all A-pluses, but neither is it all failures or disappointments. Most of the time life has a sprinkling of good moments and not-so-good moments Sunday through Saturday.

How can a person find contentment in opposing moments—both those that lend themselves to contentment and those that do not? How can one be content when they receive a pay raise *or* when they lose a job? What if age forty, sixty or eighty rolls around and life doesn't go as planned? How is contentment seeded into an established life?

The arduous and faceted journey to contentment contains times of pleasure and times of pain, changes in status, and a parade of people—some cranky, some nice—who come and go over a lifetime. Challenging aspects of life can certainly gimp the day, but only if we allow it.

This study embarks on an internal make-over because contentment arises from the inside out. Satisfaction with the moments in any given day and acceptance of surroundings comes from our loving Father, who fine tunes contentment throughout our lifetimes.

- Some are quick learners.
- Some learn slowly.
- Most are works in progress until a last breath is drawn.

Rely on God to Guide

After church one Sunday, my daughter Sheryle heard a repetitive, very loud little-boy-voice outside. Checking on two-year-old Jack, she saw he had climbed the ladder onto their trampoline and was bouncing as high as his twenty-two pounds could propel him. As he zoomed skyward, he shouted, "Jesus! Jesus!"

Sheryle asked what he was doing, and Jack said, "I'm trying to get Jesus to hear me." She explained to Jack that there was no need to shout because God even hears one's thoughts and whispers.

When we present a willing heart God listens and leads us to him. He will bring us nearer and nearer to the contentment that the Father, Son, and Spirit have among themselves. The Bible brims with stories of God and his placement of men and women into his service. And those people found more contentment in God's destinations and new commissions than in their former lives.

God called the reluctant Jonah, and even in his defiance God protected and guided. The belly of a giant fish became an altar of prayer—and a spiritual contentment rose from Jonah's lips. Even though he remained near the heartbeat of a fish, Jonah thrilled to be once again in the courts of God, again in fellowship with the Creator. An encounter with a whale-load of stomach acids and God of earth, sky, and seas, helped Jonah determine to seek that pulpit position in Nineveh after all—much more contentment there than in rebellion.

I doubt that Moabite Ruth knew when she married into the Israelite family that many personal losses lay ahead—her father-in-law, her brother-in-law, and her own dear husband died leaving her without children. But God guided the believing Ruth and her mother-in-law Naomi back to the land of promise. And there, Ruth—described by the village women "as better than seven sons"—became the wife of Boaz and the mother of Obed. God placed her in the lineage of Christ, her name forever linked with his genealogy. Ruth—reshaped, remade, recovered. God involves himself in guiding us to better places, to places of trust and contentment.

Even though we falter, stumble, forget, and whine, God understands our frailties and keeps in the lead. In a beautiful metaphor, God speaks of his careful attention to the worn out people of Israel: "I carried you on eagles' wings and brought you to myself" (Exod. 19:4). Our journeys are suited to bring us nearer to God, a place to learn contentment.

Defining Contentment

I define inward peace this way: *Contentment learned from our trustworthy God brings satisfaction of mind and heart in feast or famine.*

Christ-followers have Holy Spirit help to practice satisfaction with their portion in life whether we experience riches or poverty because God indwells and satisfies believers. "Keep your lives free from the love of money and be content with what you have, because God has said, 'Never will I leave you; never will I forsake you'" (Heb. 13:5). Again and again in holy text, God makes similar requests of detachment from this world's treasures, and he promises always to be our supplier and constant companion.

Secure in these promises, disciples of Christ can quiet their souls like a weaned child. We can accept our circumstances or seek changes, calling and waiting upon God to alter our parameters. Whether or not change takes place, asking, seeking, and knocking on the holy ground of God's waiting room is worthwhile.

Paul wrote a trust-statement encouraging Timothy: "But if we have food and clothing, we will be content with that" (1 Tim. 6:8). Jesus Christ often assured his followers that God attends to all needs, and in his prayer modeled for the disciples he requested only enough bread for the current day. When we follow Jesus' model, we ask for Monday-bread. Satisfied that God hears that request, we need not worry about the supplies in the Tuesday-pantry. God keeps our needs for Tuesday, Wednesday, and Thursday on his radar.

 A contented person can bless God for Monday-bread and say, "It is enough."

"It is enough"

In Colonial times, beds had no box springs to hold up mattresses. Instead, ropes crisscrossed underneath to support a straw or cornhusk filled ticking. Praise works like that undergirding of ropes. From here on earth, our praise supports the learning of godly contentment. Praise affirms God's attention toward us and reminds us not to worry.

During Vacation Bible School at my home church, we studied the life of Moses. Each day in the auditorium, adult volunteers acted out a series of skits about this leader of Israel. On corresponding days the stage crew produced a burning bush, manna, and a rock that gushed water. In the rock-and-water scene, a large lightweight rock formation sat on the carpeted, raised podium, complete with a small hidden tub to catch the flow. A water hose connected to an outside faucet supplied the miraculous water.

When Moses, also known as Dale Sellers, struck the rock, right on cue the water gushed out. The narrator continued the story while the thirsty Israelites gathered around to drink. With the reservoir tub about to spill over, Moses said in a slightly elevated voice, "It is enough."

Apparently the outdoor-faucet-man—at least two hundred feet away—didn't hear him. Moses increased his volume: "It is enough." But the keeper-of-the-faucet continued to bless the auditorium carpet with water. The poor Israelites lapped up as much as they could.

Finally, Moses lifted his staff and hands high above his head. He cried out in booming base, "LORD . . . IT IS ENOUGH!"

The message went through, and streams in the desert dried up.

Long-time members of the congregation still giggle about that scene, but it provided me with one of my favorite praises: "It is enough." My husband and I are self-employed, and on the worst days we may not earn enough to pay for a book of stamps. But still, on that day, we had food to eat and clothing to wear. Because God knows about that meager day, I bless him and say, "It is enough."

On other days, work pours in, and I feel like the actor Moses calling "off" God's abundance as I say at the end of those days, "Lord, today you over-blessed. Thank you. It is enough."

On days when business is poor, I sometimes hesitate to sacrifice a praise of satisfaction. And on the days when God opens the windows of heaven our way, I am humbled by his care.

Too many times on this journey toward contentment, I have trusted in my plans instead of God's. That's when God swoops down and catches this fledgling, this sparrow who still takes tumbles. The eighty-fourth psalm has long been a favorite of mine, especially this phrase, "Even the sparrow has found a home, and the swallow a nest for herself, where she may have her young—a place near your altar, O LORD Almighty, my King and my God." The psalmist continues, "Blessed are those who dwell in your house, they are ever praising you" (vv. 3-4).

Often the boundary lines of our particular lives fall in pleasant places (Ps. 16:6), but at other times suffocating sorrow envelops us. I ache to nest beside his altar to seek and receive the quieting from the One who soothes from within. Come along with me. Together, we can experience the nurturing, caring treatment of the Lord.

⟨❦⟩

Embracing Contentment
Greg Cumming's Story

Wedged into the crack between the glass doors of the church where I preached, I found two dirty white envelopes—each addressed to God in the scrawled handwriting of a child. I felt a little funny opening God's mail, but I did.

Written on the outside of the first envelope, "To the Wonderful Lord. From April To God. (Love you, Love you)." The letter, written in orange crayon with correct spelling, boasted a mixture of cursive and printing: "Dear God. I just wanted to say I love you and I will come to church next Sunday NO matter what it takes." She even wrote "Excuse me" next to a scratched-out error. She continued with, "P.S. Please write if you can. Love, April. (go to back)" On the other side, she finished, "If you write back, leave it in front of the metal church. Leave Nicole's here too." Below that, she had drawn a heart with these words inside, "I love you very very much."

Nicole addressed her envelope, "From Nicole. To God. 77049. Love you." Her neat handwriting—in pencil—revealed typical grade school spelling errors and little punctuation. But, I doubt God cared. She wrote, "Dear God Do you have a minute I have something to tell you it is real importent I have cursed a cuople times But now I am strighting my act up Write back to me Leave it in front of the metal church with Aprils I love you By: Nicole Love you"

As far as I know, despite April's determination, nobody ever brought the girls to church. However, I did meet the girl cousins on two occasions. Believe me, you don't want to know their stories. Suffice it to say we live in a monstrously evil world with wicked family secrets. Even though I made reports to Child Protective Services, no one responded to my pleas for help.

By now April and Nichole are around thirty years of age, probably with children of their own. I wonder if the cousins overcame their circumstances or if they remain trapped in the same quagmire? I consider the possible differences it could have made if their parents had brought them to the metal church.

I saved their letters and think of the girls now and then. I weep for them. I pray for the women they've become. Even though I didn't see answers to my earlier prayers, I trust that God will once again stir their longing to talk with him—to seek him.

As a husband, dad, granddad, and minister, I've encountered many things out of my power to heal or mend. But I've found contentment in trusting God, who remains larger than all the circumstances I try to fix.

After all, he is a genuine father, and he read April's and Nichole's prayers long before I did.

Memorize and offer these prayers to still and quiet your soul.

Praise: "I lie down and sleep; I wake again, because the LORD sustains me" (Ps. 3:5).

Petition: "I have sought your face with all my heart; be gracious to me according to your promise" (Ps. 119:58).

As you consider the questions, remember:

- Spending time with God allows him to quiet your soul.
- Contentment is learned.
- Contentment is satisfaction of mind and heart in any circumstance.
- Praise undergirds contentment.

1. *"Contentment learned from our trustworthy God brings satisfaction of mind and heart in feast or famine."* Contemplate your level of contentment. Are you content in all things? In what area(s) do you struggle with contentment?

2. It's easy to be contented on days when everything remains harmonious, but how do you quiet your soul, and get back to

that place of contentment on days when worries—either real or imagined—invade?

3. Can haughty eyes be a sign of self sufficiency? Explain.

4. God is ultra-capable of sustaining his creation. How big is the God you serve? Do you fully trust him to be the keeper of your life? How does your life reflect this?

5. In Colossians 1:29, Paul wanted to present—as a gift to God—his fellow travelers "perfect in Christ Jesus." Christ's energy working powerfully in him was a key to success. Write down some ways Christ's energy works through you.

6. God promises, "Never will I leave you. Never will I forsake you" (Heb. 13:5). How is this truth embedded in your heart? In your actions? In your thought life?

7. Recall a time you actually witnessed a child's trust in God? Recall a time when you witnessed another adult exhibiting childlike trust?

8. Word a simple praise and prayer asking God to wean you from chronic worry and bring you to fully trust his complete care.

Chapter Two

CLIFF DWELLING

Draw Near to God on the Journey

There is a place near me where you may stand on a rock.

Exodus 33:21, God speaking to Moses

Most mornings my husband gets up readying for work long before daylight—from midnight to 4:00 A.M.—and I get up and prepare a brown bag lunch for him. Depending on the hour, I remain up or lie down for a bit more sleep. One morning, he left near 3:00 A.M., and I stayed up for an hour to finish leftover chores. I unloaded the dishwasher and tidied up the house—not calculus, so my thoughts soon abandoned the mundane tasks.

While I cleared countertops, I planned the content of my next newspaper column. Moving from room to room, my hands kept busy dusting and sweeping while my brainwaves crashed against distant shores. When I floated back to the moment, I looked down at our bed and found the sheet corners tucked and comforter in place. I like to consider myself industrious, but I had planned to rest a few more hours so the sun and I could get up at the same time.

My mind often drifts while I am performing routines and my inattention on that early morning reminded me of the days when I wander around disturbed by the mayhem in my world and the world at large. Life is full of distractions, but cliff dwelling with God can draw us near to him and his gracious benefit of contentment. Later in this chapter, we'll consider Moses' request to know God and how God answered, "Yes."

Each Unique Life— God's Training Ground toward Contentment

We each experience unique backgrounds made up of childhood and later experiences. Our stories—numberless as blades of grass—have distinctive DNA, made up from our heritage, our choices, our work, and our family and friends. Through both fertile and dry seasons we can learn contentment if we choose to cliff-dwell with God. Whether young in years and faith, mid-lifers, or Christian fossils, we can choose to embrace contentment.

In this chapter, I'll fill you in on what helped me move toward the level of contentment I now experience. I'll also share how God, along the way, watered my life with the Word, his Holy Spirit, and his ever-present help when life withered.

Why am I writing about contentment? As I've contemplated the phases of my life so far, I know God has groomed me every day toward more contentment. Many needy people surround me, but I experience more peace than ever before because Jesus Christ's all-surpassing power continues to surprise and support me.

All-Surpassing Power

The Apostle Paul described his ministry of reflecting the Lord's glory even through trials. He praised the light of Jesus reflected in his and his co-workers' hearts, calling it an "all-surpassing power"—spiritual power in dust-made bodies. Because of God's indwelling, Paul recognized that tough places can be filled with hope: "We are hard pressed on every side, but not crushed; perplexed, but not in despair; persecuted, but not abandoned; struck down, but not destroyed" (2 Cor. 4:7-8). Now that's explicit contentment.

Over the span of a life, most will face one or more experiences similar to Paul's persecutions—hard pressed, perplexed, or struck down. But just as God infused hope into Paul's ministry, God ably reproduces that same hope in us, assuring us of his power and presence. When I hear the group L'Angelus sing "Tantum Ergo," I'm always moved by this translated phrase, "Faith will tell us Christ is present when our human senses fail." As we live and move in God's presence, he provides us with the same "all-surpassing power" of Christ, which in turn yields godly contentment.

Contentment Training—My Story

I was born with a plastic spoon in my mouth. My dad and mom worked hard to provide for us, and they often went without so their children could succeed. Their devotion to God and family laid a solid foundation for my budding faith to grow.

Self employed since early marriage, my husband and I work long hours, some of which involve manual labor. Of course I now have an air conditioned office in my home, but I'm not always able to accomplish all my work from my comfy swivel chair.

I blew out sixty-two birthday candles this year and celebrated forty-three years of marriage to my godly husband, David. God gave us a son and daughter, and increased our family through their Christian spouses and five grandchildren, who all live near us. Both sets of our parents are alive and live within fifteen miles of our home. My dad still drives and lives in his home. My mother suffers from end-stage Parkinson's disease in a nursing facility. My husband's parents live in their home and a caretaker drives them and helps out three days a week. Our siblings are terrific, but with our more flexible schedules and proximity, David and I enjoy the blessing of helping our parents with their daily needs.

For now, we have no plans for retirement—full or partial. Add to caring for our parents, our marriage and Saturday night dates, children and grandchildren, church family, worship, and my passion to write, speak and teach, and our lives remain full.

Pauses

In the early days of our self employment we erected metal buildings—barns, airplane hangars, and work shops for businesses. We had two employees, hubby and me. That's when God trained me to accept every-day "pauses." I call those unexpected, not-on-the-to-do-list happenings "pauses," but they often became the catalyst for learning contentment. Accepting the delays in my day helped me to learn satisfaction. If one of our trucks broke down, I paused my current project and trekked after parts.

A change in plans became the norm for our family. We finally hired a Saturday helper, but if he didn't show up, I packed our toddlers' lunches, turned off the cartoons, and helped put up one more steel building.

My steel-worker "job description" also moved me far away from my comfort zone in the area of work skills. I often drove our winch truck to the job site, pulling a gooseneck trailer loaded with steel and topped with a Porta-Crib.

At the job site, I sometimes operated the winch truck. Some locations had steep inclines near the foundations, too steep for me to back our winch truck up to a building to deliver roofing tin. A truck clutch and my foot just aren't that compatible. So on the days when we roofed a building with sheet iron, Dave operated the winch truck and I took the position of ladder-helper.

The bundle of roofing tin had a heavy-duty strap in the middle and a lead rope around one end of the bundle. To begin, I would stand on the ground holding the end of the rope. As I climbed the ladder toward the eave of the building, the rope enabled me to keep the sheet iron level as Dave operated the truck winch and hoisted the bundle of tin toward the roof purlin.

Was I uncomfortable when I climbed a tall ladder, holding a lead rope, gripping each ladder rung on my ascent to the eave? Absolutely. But I also knew great joy when I descended and found my head still attached to my neck.

Would I have preferred to be a full-time, stay-at-home mom—maybe. But that wasn't the life God had called me to.

I confess to being exasperated, cranky, or ill-tempered on job sites at times. Little by little, and I do mean small increments at a time, God guided me to give thanks for our work and to become content. Because of his constant, faithful Spirit I could smile more while landing tin, rejoice while baking our favorite cookies, and not get too ruffled when "pauses" dotted my days. Throughout the process, God groomed me toward satisfaction with my life and work. Each day, each turn, each incident became a unique training ground where contentment could grow.

We eventually moved from that business to the trucking business where I learned new skills, but I will not, cannot, should not drive semitrucks. My husband says there are truck drivers (those who understand the mechanics of a truck) and "steering wheel holders." I qualify only for the latter.

Why do I share my work history with you? Because in those years of daily schedule changes and areas where I wasn't comfortable working, that chameleon life helped me learn contentment. I am a more contented wife, mother, grandmother, daughter, daughter-in-law, and caretaker at this stage of life because of that early training ground.

Alongside the physical work, I had many quiet cliff-dwelling moments with God when he trained, comforted, and soothed me to contentment. Sometimes, those took place in the early morning at home, before I awakened our son and daughter. Or on job sites, I could read or study during a lull while David welded purlin on the roof trusses. Those moments of allowing God's word to be engraved upon my heart still brace my courage to live out my faith today.

His Holy Spirit still keeps my spirit from destruction and despair. Like Paul, I do not fear abandonment because God has a track record, etched in my life.

Moses' Cliff Dwelling

Seeking to capture and hold on to contentment, I've asked myself throughout the years, "With what am I satisfied, filled up, fulfilled, and happiest?" My answers tell me that I can be happy with a job I don't particularly enjoy. I can be satisfied with my current possessions, or even fewer dishtowels, trinkets, and shoes. But another question pops into my mind with regularity: Could I be content with what I know about God up to this time in my life? As long as I'm able-minded, I hope to seek God to more fully comprehend him.

Even past the age of eighty, Moses yearned to understand more of God and on one occasion made this request, "If I have found favor in your eyes, teach me your ways so that I may know you and continue to find favor with you" (Exod. 33:13).

God responded. Can you imagine? That God responds to Moses' requests inspires awe. In the complete scene, the eventual conversation between God and Moses becomes one of the most poignant in their history. Read God's response to Moses' request: "There is a place near me where you may stand on a rock. When my glory passes by, I will put you in a cleft in the rock and cover you with my hand until I have passed by. Then I will remove my hand and you will see my back; but my face must not be seen" (Exod. 33:21-23).

Moses—living in the ninth decade of his life—has heard, seen, and interacted with God as much or more than the patriarchs Abraham, Isaac, and Jacob. He and the Israelites experienced God's unprecedented care and manifestation, but Moses' deep desire remained—to know more about God. He craved closeness to the heart of God, not just proximity.

Near God Is Solid Ground

The words God spoke to Moses put goose-bumps on my soul: "There is a place near me where you may stand on a rock." I don't write a lot of fiction, but when I'm working on a scene, I sometimes act it out or picture in my mind how it might play out on a movie screen. Imagine the incredible moments between Moses and God. God is not distant. He is near, very near, and God told Moses that he could stand on solid ground. This symbolizes, for me, God as bedrock foundation. A lot of sand-shifting will happen over the course of a life, and bedrock is the solid rock that underlies loose material, such as soil, sand, clay, or gravel—or broken relationships, illnesses, or dusty faith.

This meeting between God and Moses reveals another key to learning contentment—intimate moments with God. In addition to our unique personal training grounds, we learn and secure contentment through fellowship with God. Following Moses' request, God chose a place for their meeting—a summit for two.

Today, quiet time-slots with God offset the times when life rushes along like an interstate. God ably teaches me on six-lane roads, as well as dirt roads in remote areas. However, contemplating God on a freeway versus a quiet country lane is as different as tornadoes and tranquility.

Life continually allures with a plastic bouquet of distractions, but God longs for real, fragrant, intimate meetings. Whenever I experience friendly moments with God, he extends a peace-blessing which enables me to stand on his absolute promises: "You will keep in perfect peace him whose mind is steadfast, because he trusts in you" (Isa. 26:3). For trust and contentment to grow:

- We need God's solid ground, not the world's quicksand.
- We need the sameness found in God, not the world's fluctuation.
- We need God's trusted promises, not the world's pledges.

Do you want to stand on The Rock instead of quaking ground? If you want your contentment to advance, adopt Moses' request and write it on an index card. Display it as a prompt to pray: "Teach me your ways so that I may know you and continue to find favor with you" (Exod. 33:13).

Humility and Contentment

Throughout Moses' unique life, God shaped him into a humble man, a man contented to let God rule in his life: "Now Moses was a very humble man, more humble than anyone else on the face of the earth" (Num. 12:3). Moses' life presented a variety of moments in which humility incubated. His history is rich with stories of his family's devotion, being reared with royalty, tending sheep for forty years, and living a Bedouin life. He saw a flame retardant bush and heard the voice of God. And at the geriatric age of eighty, God's plan for the rest of his life unfolded. He had another forty years to live and work as the shepherd of a huge, sometimes rowdy flock.

Rabbi David Wolpe explains humility and describes Moses' renown as the most humble man on earth:

> Of all the remarkable qualities of Moses, one is singled out for mention in the Torah—Moses was the most humble man on earth. (Num. 12:3)
>
> Genuine humility is not the absence of self-esteem. They are actually the same.
>
> Esteem of oneself comes less from qualities than from essence—not simply what we do but who we understand ourselves to be. Genuine self-esteem mandates that I feel badly about myself at times, for I have acted in a way not worthy of the soul I was given. A great musician will reproach himself for mistakes in performance that a lesser artist would ignore. As we grow in soul we have more occasions to scrutinize ourselves and our conduct. To feel always good about oneself is to set the bar distressingly low.

Moses was humbled before the Creator of the universe. Understanding God better than any man who ever lived, he appreciated the relative position of human and Divine in the cosmos. His accomplishments grew from his character; he knew his place in the world as a leader and teacher; he was not falsely modest. Moses' esteem grew from being in God's image and his humility from understanding how infinitely greater is the Original than the image.[1]

Confident humility settled deep into Moses' heart because he had genuine answers through his relationship with God to the great questions of life: "Where did I come from?" "Why am I here?" and "Where am I going?" The world comes up short on ways to live a full life. Philosophies of men offer no meaningful response to the questions most people eventually ask themselves. The real answers to life's tough questions come only when Jesus, the heart muscle of God, becomes Lord of our lives.

He Covers Me There with His Hand

"A Wonderful Savior," one of Fanny J. Crosby's stirring hymns, always reminds me of chapters 33 and 34 of Exodus, the cliff dwelling scene. My favorite line from the song is, "He hideth my soul in the cleft of the rock and covers me there with his hand." I imagine Moses standing on solid rock and God offering further protection as he leads Moses away from the ledge, protectively places him in the crevice of the mountain, and covers him with his hand.

Despite many physical difficulties, Frances Jane Crosby (1820-1915) allowed God to lead her to contentment. She lost her sight in her first year on earth. Later, she didn't allow bitterness about her disability to rule her attitude. Some accurately said about her loss of sight, "But her heart can see." Over her lifetime, she wrote at least one thousand hymns using about one hundred pseudonyms because publishers didn't believe that one person's work should take up so much space in a hymnal. At a mature age Mrs. Crosby said, "If perfect earthly sight were offered me tomorrow I would not accept it. I might not have sung hymns to the praise of God if I had been distracted by the beautiful and interesting things about me."[2] Even at the age of eight, she had comfortably settled into her sightless world and she wrote this poem:

> Oh what a happy soul I am,
> Although I cannot see;
> I am resolved that in this world
> Contented I will be.
> How many blessings I enjoy,
> That other people don't;
> To weep and sigh because I'm blind,
> I cannot, and I won't.[3]

Like Moses, Mrs. Crosby embraced her life-role. When singing the words to "A Wonderful Savior," I'm carried away to the crevice where God continually hides me. I cannot help but cup my right hand over my left and bless God for the many times he sets me on solid rock, to bless God for covering me with the precious blood of Jesus, for seeding contentment in my heart.

As we embrace our unique places in life, we can allow God to be our teacher. He will tutor us toward humility. He will place us on solid ground near him. May he grow our peace so that the emaciated world, feasting upon quick fixes and temporary satisfactions, will see our souls fat with contentment and long to feast with us at God's table.

Embracing Contentment
Judy Martin Bowyer's Story

As a tribute to John Steinbeck, I call 1973 the "winter of our discontent." My excursion into wifehood still had training wheels attached. We moved to Dallas, where we knew almost no one, and my husband worked long hours, leaving me home with a toddler in training pants. We had agreed I would stay at home with our son, but some days that seemed like a really poor choice.

We were involved in a good church and began meeting couples our age. Unfortunately, the church campus was located in upper middle class Dallas, which meant most of our new acquaintances seemed on a fast track to success.

The comparisons between "them" and "us" began to gnaw at me. My husband and I shared a vehicle—a beat-up Volkswagen with two different color fenders. Because our car had no air conditioner on our summer Sunday drives to church, we arrived sweat-stained, only to park beside the line up of shiny BMWs and Cadillacs.

We rented a small apartment while most of the church members owned houses with three or four bedrooms. None of our church family seemed to mind where we lived, but I became increasingly discontent with what we didn't have.

While potty training our toddler, laundry seemed to multiply. Because my husband drove the car to work, I had to walk uphill carrying overloaded baskets to reach the laundromat. Every step of the way, I sent out invitations to my very own pity party. "If only we had a washer and dryer, I would be happy."

I didn't keep my lamentations to myself, either. I made sure my husband knew how miserable I was. By voicing my desire, I certainly didn't intend to slam him. Still, he couldn't help but feel as though my complaints were a personal attack on his ability to provide adequately for us.

With each passing day, I agonized about how deprived I felt with no washer and dryer. My wants became a single-minded focus. All of life's frustrations and my sense of inferiority boiled up and became centered, oddly enough, on the washer/dryer issue. Of course, the lack of my own laundry appliances had little to do with the real issue.

Fortunately, God got my attention. I finally understood that my obsession had gotten out of control. I wanted to abandon my mistaken belief that owning a washer and dryer would bring me happiness.

One night, as my husband worked his late shift, I put our son to bed and sat in the living room. Turning off all the lights, I sat in the dark, staring into the nothingness. "God, are you there? I need you!" I cried aloud. I didn't know what to ask for, but I knew I could not fix this problem by myself.

"Lord, I don't want to be so materialistic. I know that doesn't please you. I know I've been wrong to want 'things' more than I want you. I'm out of control and making myself miserable. Please take away this lust for material things," I begged aloud.

Then I felt the Holy Spirit urging me to do something that is somewhat foreign to my church background. I slowly and deliberately raised my hands to the ceiling, stretching with all my might toward God. A sense of freedom broke loose inside me as I grasped for a physical connection to God. I poured out my heart again.

"I can't do this alone; I can only give up my selfish 'wants' if you help me," I sobbed. "Help me be content no matter what I have or don't have. I promise not to bug you about the washer and dryer until you are ready to give them to me."

I felt an almost physical sensation of God grasping my hands, during which he soothed my troubled spirit with the oil of his peace. I had finally "let go" and put my situation in his hands in a way I had never done before.

That evening marked a spiritual turning point for me—one in which I found new strength to wrestle with everyday stresses. We didn't suddenly grow richer, but we eventually became very close friends with other couples at church, and we were accepted without regard to our financial status.

The washer-dryer era certainly wasn't the only time I struggled with materialistic wants or felt distant from God, but it became one of those "drive a stake in the ground" moments I return to again and again. It helps me remember that

God's faithfulness grants me peace and contentment when I ask him, when I let go of those "it's all about me" cravings.

These days, as I look back through the lens of a more mature faith, my fixation on having a washer/dryer borders the comical. Why was that such a life-or-death goal for me? It had assumed epic proportions in my mind.

Almost four decades later, I'm still on my journey. And like Paul, I continue to learn how to "be content whatever the circumstances."

Memorize and pray these scriptures as you draw near to God on your journey.

Praise: "We give thanks to you, O God, we give thanks, for your Name is near" (Ps. 75:1).
Petition: "Teach me your way, O LORD, and I will walk in your truth; give me an undivided heart, that I may fear your name" (Ps. 86:11).

As you consider the questions, remember:

- Your life is a unique classroom for learning contentment.
- Christ's all-surpassing power enables your contentment.
- "Pauses" happen.
- Cliff-dwelling with God provides solid ground.
- Humility is a seedbed for contentment.

1. Sketch a timeline of your life, naming five significant events from birth to present. How did your contentment grow through these events?
2. Often we manage large scale life-happenings with grace. How do you react in thought and actions when your day "pauses"?
3. In 2 Corinthians 4:7 Paul applauded an "all surpassing power" found in God and described his difficulties as "light and momentary troubles" (v. 17). How do you answer to difficulties? Name a specific

trial and your response. Name one difficulty you viewed as a "light and momentary" trouble?

4. Paul said he and his companions fixed their eyes "not on what is seen, but on what is unseen" (2 Cor. 4:18). Recall and write a brief account of a recent time when you diverted your attention from the temporary in this life to the unseen hand of God.

5. How often do you cliff dwell with God—read the Bible, meditate, or pray? What do you need to change, eliminate, or rearrange in your life to give you more time with your Father?

6. How often do you crave closeness to God? Can you recall a specific time in your life when your spirit fully knew that God was near, loving you, protecting you?

7. Where is your quicksand? How do you reclaim solid ground near God?

8. "But he gives us more grace. That is why Scripture says: 'God opposes the proud but gives grace to the humble'" (James 4:6; Prov. 3:34). Where in your life does pride reign? Word a simple prayer giving that area over to God, expecting to receive humility and learn contentment.

Chapter Three

SPIRIT WILT

Complaining Sabotages Contentment

Do everything without complaining....
Philippians 2:14

"Ain't it Awful!" Before we ever reached home, our nine-year-old daughter, Sheryle, read the title to her Sunday school chart aloud to our family. She explained that we were to use a graph she received by recording who complained and how many times. When we arrived at our house, she penciled in her name, "Daddy," "Mom," and "Russell" (her brother's name). She vowed to keep tabs on all our complaints.

I thought to myself, *I'll monitor the kiddos too. This chart will help them see how often they whine.* Within a couple of hours, I whimpered about my hair and the South Texas humidity. My young daughter Sheryle whipped out her chart pronouncing loudly, "Ain't it awful!" She promptly put a check by my name and proclaimed, "You're the first to complain."

Ouch—a pine tree in my eye and pine pollen in hers. Timber! I was reminded to first look at my habit of complaining before scouting for family's offenses.

In this chapter, we'll examine how our grumbling and complaining sabotages our relationship with God and consider practical training methods that focus on God's help in getting rid of whining and replacing it with praise. Simply pointing out complaining isn't enough because most people can adequately spot grumbling. I hope to assist in derailing complaining and offer assurance that when we lift our voices to the Lord he hears and helps entrench contentment.

Complaint Department

Retail stores used to have a service called a "Complaint Department." Clerks manned a station where disgruntled shoppers could discuss issues. Most stores no longer have those departments, though some have re-named them "Customer Service." That name has a more positive ring and really identifies the store's goal of customer retention because they trust that store to treat their requests in a fair manner.

Complaining just to be complaining is like spinning wheels in deep mud—you work hard and go nowhere; you don't get to a better place. Finding fault can become chronic. A habitual whiner can find one wrong in twenty-five "rights," and rarely gets through a conversation without identifying something amiss in relationships or politics or the world.

What should really bother us—the little things that go wrong in our days or larger issues in life? Do we get distracted by the rust, the decay, the spills and splats, allowing dozens—or hundreds—of annoyances to take root in our hearts? Let's examine the domino effects of complaining.

Complaint Siblings

Complaining to friends, family, and even people you've just met can result in a bad side effect: the habit of complaining spreads to others. Before you can say, "Forgive me for whining," the other person may have caught the ill spirit of complaining. This communicable disease can create complaint siblings.

When my children were young, I fashioned flashcard scriptures from poster board, with a scripture on one side and the same scripture depicted in rebus on the opposite side. One of their scriptures was a familiar verse in Philippians 2:14 that says to do *all* things without murmuring or complaining. Last time I checked, the word "all" meant one hundred percent. That's a notable goal, to encounter each day's events knowing that things will go awry, and with a determination not to be caught off guard, surprised, or prone to complain when something negative happens.

Do you know a constant complainer, whiner, or moaner? My grandma called steady complaints bellyaching. It doesn't take too long to grow weary of a faultfinder's company. I saw a gazebo beside a lake in the back yard of a lovely home, readily used to entertain Christians, host baptisms, baby and wedding showers, and Bible study groups. As I attended an event there one day, I noticed buzzards roosting on their gazebo.

"Buzzard" is the southern term for vulture. Buzzards eat dead things. The stark contrast between idyllic gazebo and buzzards gave me a clear picture of the ugliness of whining that roosts in souls. For a moment think of your pet peeves, your top two annoyances. I tend to get annoyed when people over explain something to me, or when a telemarketer tries to send a fax to my cell phone.

How do you respond to your list of irritants? Little things will go wrong each day, and if we continue to respond with complaints, that nasty habit can embed and fester in our spirits and then spread into the community of people around us.

I was with a group of folk at a great restaurant when one person told about a slightly bad meal at another eating establishment. All of a sudden, more of our group brought up former negative dining experiences—wait staff, food prep, or prices—and for ten minutes we whined and dined while a lovely meal sat before us. My friend Leslie Wilson calls this social one-upmanship. And we were trying to out-complain each other!

A classic example of complaining is the nation of Israel. These newly liberated slaves found themselves in a staggering transitional stage of their lives. For years, God laid the groundwork to remove them from harsh taskmasters and subservience to freedom. When the time was right, God moved them out of Egypt. Though Israel had visual sightings of his presence in a pillar of fire and a guiding cloud, constant whining and complaining about their situation permeated the culture of these freed slaves. And, much like my dining experience, the rescued slaves neglected thanksgiving and their complaints spread causing the community to grumble.

After all God implemented for Israel, "[T]hey despised the pleasant land; they did not believe his promise. They grumbled in their tents and did not obey the LORD" (Ps. 106:24-25). Despising the pleasant territory where we dwell and failing to believe God's promises equals a session of family-tent-grumbling. How many times do my eyes fail to perceive bounty because, like Israel, I look at presumed barricades?

God gave Moses a song to teach to Israel, and some of the lyrics haunt my soul for I also complain about my blessings: "[Israel] grew fat and kicked; filled with food, he became heavy and sleek. He abandoned the God who made him and rejected the Rock his Savior" (Deut. 32:15). The song, taught to Israel at God's command, reminds Israel of their forgetfulness. For me, the lyric-picture reveals a domestic animal bellying up to a full trough of food. I see the animal kick against the master as he approaches to shovel in more grain. That's complaining. Prosperity, pride, and stubborn self-will line the path to forgetting God. Israel's complaining eventually led to idolatry—for it is man's nature to worship—but in their initial steps they forgot their maker and supplier.

Grumbling begets complaint siblings. We see it in our homes, in school rooms, in political parties, in our neighborhoods, and in nations. Complaining undermines contentment. Complaining causes a lot of sighing in those who have to listen to it day after day. They tire of our presence. Chronic moaning will cause people to tune us out because constant whining disheartens.

But what if you have a legitimate complaint? Or what if you are just in a funk and can't get out? Who can you turn to? Who will listen and not sigh or grow weary?

Tell God, Not Your Companions

"I pour out my complaint before him; before him I tell my trouble. When my spirit grows faint within me, it is you who know my way" (Ps. 142:2). When something goes wrong and it will, the best thing we can do is to tell God. But if we make a habit of fault-finding within a community of people—family, church, friends—we run the risk of infecting them with our cantankerous spirit. It's like the flu, spread from person to person and very contagious. All who come in contact are susceptible to the spreading disease.

The opposite of frail humans, God ably listens to both our concerns and non-viable complaints with no damage to his nature. When we voice injustices—real or perceived—to God, he has the power to do something about them. From minor mishaps to major hurts, God's trademark is listening, whether we have a miserable case of poison ivy or suffer emotional distress because of relationships or a prodigal child.

The prophet Jeremiah even complained to God about God. He blamed God for making him grow old, for keeping him in the dark, for surrounding him with bitterness and hardship. He accused God of weighing him down with chains and of imitating a lion lying in wait, who dragged him from the path and mangled him (Lam. 3). Very heavy accusations.

Jeremiah didn't stop there. He lamented that his teeth were broken because of chewing on gravel. He also implied that God had drawn a bull's eye on his back and used him for target practice. His mind toiled on negative happenings and his soul was downcast.

But God pours out his grace to our inward spirits even when we dump wrath, anger, and disappointment into his lap. He doesn't reciprocate in kind. Instead, he gifts his hurting children with total understanding. Psalm 103 depicts God as one who "redeems my life from the pit" and who "knows how we are formed, he remembers that we are dust" (vv. 4, 14). Even through our fits of God-blaming and whining, God infuses hope and focuses the complainer's attention upon God's constancy and goodness. He rescues us from poor-me spirits.

Jeremiah went through some horrible times, but hope nudged its way into his grumbling-tent when he recalled the true character of God, not his skewed human version. "Yet this I call to mind and therefore I have hope: Because of the LORD's great love we are not consumed, for his compassions never fail." He continues with a sunrise statement about God's mercies: "They are new every morning; great is your faithfulness." And he finishes with a training exercise: "I say to myself, 'The LORD is my portion; therefore I will wait for him'" (Lam. 3:21-24).

Allow God to turn your heart toward him by reviewing your habits of complaining and praise.

- Complaining destroys impetus for praise.
- Turn whining over to God.
- God gives new mercies every morning.

What training exercises help us focus on the true character of God instead of just what our eyes see? Let's explore those.

Hope

It's easy to identify bad habits that I would rather not have in my life, but the more difficult thing is establishing a training regimen to eliminate those destructive patterns—behaviors which are contrary to God's character. Too often we're lazy runners in the Christian race. Drifters. Complacent. We might want to be more disciplined but we are not willing to put forth the effort to reach goals. *The Message*—in contemporary language—convicts and challenges lethargic Christians:

> You've all been to the stadium and seen the athletes race. Everyone runs; one wins. Run to win. All good athletes train hard. They do it for a gold medal that tarnishes and fades. You're after one that's gold eternally.

I don't know about you, but I'm running hard for the finish line. I'm giving it everything I've got. No sloppy living for me! I'm staying alert and in top condition. I'm not going to get caught napping, telling everyone else all about it and then missing out myself. (1 Cor. 9:24-27)

Each day Paul trained and raced toward a goal. He wanted to win his race, not for personal recognition, but because he campaigned for Jesus. I shudder to think how little I've trained myself not to complain. Some days I do well, but on other days I fail miserably. How well would you fare if your every word of complaint were measured?

We train for many things in life. We potty train toddlers, train children to clean rooms, and teach good manners and prompt children when they receive a cookie to say, "Thank you." Yet regimens for learning godliness are often the last on the list.

We train to swing bats, ride bicycles, and use computers. We take driver's education training. Musicians, laborers, artists, craftsmen, professionals—all apprentice, train, and practice to acquire and improve skills. And yet, how much thought goes into training toward godliness or wiping out chronic complaints?

Consider when we use the word "hate." Could there be any better indicator of complaining? I sometimes hear Christians say "I just hate it when the electricity is off," or "I hate guacamole with onions," or "I hate big box stores." Usually when we use the word "hate," it is in conjunction with a luxury that doesn't measure up to our high standards. We can get so caught up in making sure everything pleases us that we forget the ungratefulness conveyed in that word.

Our whims may crowd out concern for the brokenness of people, the real heartache of God. One effort I've made in training toward godliness is to wipe the word "hate" from most of my vocabulary. Do you use the word "hate" often? Increase your awareness of it, noticing the times you do use it. If so, what is the object of your hate?

That training can be taken a step further to help eliminate complaints. Try fasting—not from food—but from whining.

Fast from Complaining

Now in her eighties, Jan has grown into one of the most God-honoring and contented women I know. At her apartment one day during a writing critique session, she started to say something then stopped herself. With a twinkle in her eye, she said, "I'm fasting from complaining this week." Even during the final chapters of her life, she single-mindedly serves her Lord and maintains training.

She gifted me with a technique that I find very helpful in many areas of my life—fasting from bad habits, enabling my spirit to be regulated by God's Spirit. If you are in the habit of complaining, don't wait. Today, dedicate an hour as a non-complaint hour, in both your thoughts and words. Then tomorrow add an hour. Don't be shy if an opportunity comes up to share the exercise with someone. Your example could encourage someone's own training regimen, and you and a co-faster could encourage one another.

As we fast from complaining, God uproots dissatisfaction and replaces it with praise. During a fast, follow Jesus' example of repelling evil with scripture: be armed with a praise scripture, a prayer, or a thanksgiving to turn your mind toward blessings. When I have an urge to whine, I use this plea: "Lord, restore the joy of your salvation and the joy of obeying you." It's simple, but immediately the focus shifts from the current irritant and onto the bigger work of God.

The Shunnamite woman's non-complaining in the Old Testament is a real comfort-story to me. I taught about her in a women's class and her compliance and non-complaining gained entrance to my heart, and I've not been the same since. I'm excited to share what I learned from her, and I hope that we can capture and nourish her level of contentment in our own lives.

The Shunammite Woman

"Live carefree before God; he is most careful with you. He gets the Last Word" (1 Pet. 5:7, *The Message*). Those words could have been written about the unnamed woman from Shunem. From the brief encounter with her, it's evident she appreciated the carefulness of God directed to her and ones she loved.

When the prophet Elisha traveled through her city limits, she took notice of him and offered hospitality. Contextual clues (2 Kings 4) reveal that Elisha made a habit of stopping at her home for meals when he traveled through that region. In time, she suggested to her husband that they add on a room at the top of their home, probably balcony style. She furnished it with a bed, chair and table or desk, and an oil lamp. The room could accommodate someone for a nap or an overnight stay.

One day after resting comfortably, Elisha sent a message of thanks to his hostess through his servant Gehazi. He asked her if he could speak to the king or to the captain of the army on her behalf.

Her reply indicates contentment and no grievance about government and no favor to ask of the military: "I have a home among my own people" (v. 13). If someone offered to represent me to the head of state, would I decline? Probably not. I would want them to plead some cause for me. And I'm sure I could think of something that the military could do for me—maybe find a cushy job for my soldier-friend. But the contented Shunammite woman turned down the return-favors offered to her.

Within a short time, Elisha summoned her. She stood in the door of his room and listened as he told her the desires of her heart were a possibility. "About this time next year, you will hold a son in your arms" (v. 16).

A suppressed longing emerges from her: "No, my lord, don't mislead your servant, O man of God!" (v. 16). Up to this time, even though she longed for a child, she had faithfully used her energies to care for her husband, oversee her household, and provide lodging for the man of God and his servant.

I want to pause in the telling of her story and think about the subject of infertility, which may be one of the most difficult areas to abide in contentment. I especially got a better understanding of her childlessness and her probable emotions when considering one scene in Abram's life. In a vision, God said, "Do not be afraid, Abram. I am your shield, your very great reward" (Gen. 15:1).

Consider this: God is present and communicating with Abram. God also tells him to abandon his fears and assures him of God-shielding, and then God promises himself as Abram's reward. Astounding! All that and yet Abram replies, "O Sovereign LORD, what can you give me since I remain childless . . . . [y]ou have given me no children" (vv. 2-3).

Abram's pain surges through his reply. The density of his longing melts my heart. I have several dear friends who never had children or adopted a child. They have arrived at a place of contentment, but occasionally a specific sadness drapes their countenances, and because I know them so well, I know it surfaced because of an unmet expectation of welcoming a child into their family.

Equipped with these insights, I appreciate even more the Shunammite's service to others—of her contentment to "mother" in other ways. True to Elisha's prediction she gave birth to a son about a year later. And the mother and son story will further reveal her contentment, deep faith, and trust in God.

When the boy was old enough to go into the fields with his father during harvest, the child became ill and cried out, "My head! My head!" (2 Kings 4:19). His father instructed a servant to carry him to his mother where "[t]he boy sat on her lap until noon, and then he died" (v. 20). The narrator of 2 Kings says the mother took her son and laid him on the prophet's bed, shut the door, and went out.

She called to her husband, probably still in the field, and asked for a servant to accompany her to Mount Carmel to see the prophet. Her curious husband wondered why she wanted to make the journey because it wasn't a day set aside for worship. Determined to get to the man of God, she avoided telling her husband the sad news of their son's death, but assured him with her farewell, literally saying, "Shalom" or all is well (v. 23).

From her saddled donkey, she told the servant to lead on and not slow down unless at her command. Mount Carmel was about fifteen miles from Shunem. It probably took her until early evening to reach Elisha's home. Gehazi, the prophet's servant, met her and asked, "Is all well with you? Is all well with your husband? Is all well with your child?" (v. 26 ESV).

She answered, "All is well" (v. 26 ESV).

I don't know about you, but I can see myself falling apart at nearly any juncture in this story. When she finally reached Elisha, she fell at his feet grasping them. The man of God recognized her "bitter distress" (v. 27). Maybe that's when her emotions cratered because she knew she had come to a place of refuge, hope, and help.

She had received this son and now lost him. Her anguish is palpable: "Did I ask you for a son, my lord? Didn't I tell you, 'Don't raise my hopes'" (v. 28).

The Shunammite's compulsion to travel hours to get to the man of God, even with dense grief weighing her down is compelling. I desire that kind of trust. Her child lay dead, and yet her first thoughts and spoken words to people were, "All is well." But when she reached the man of God, she felt free to pour out her heart.

They made the return trip to Shunem where Elisha rushed to his guest room. He shut the door and prayed alone with the lifeless body of the boy stretched upon his couch. When God returned life to the boy, he sneezed seven times and opened his eyes. Perhaps God's way of letting his mother know—through that closed door—that life had returned to her little son. In gratitude, "She came in, fell at his feet and bowed to the ground" (v. 37).

Because none of us live in paradise (yet), many unpleasant things continue to happen here on earth, things that scar our souls. But if we plan and carry out a training program, we can minimize and eventually delete complaining. And if trouble lands in the heart of your family, get to God, grasp his feet, and bare your soul. That's where we experience his careful attention and learn the contentment of carefree living.

✺

Embracing Contentment
Tammy Marcelain's Story

I woke up one morning and felt like everything was right in my world. I had just finished my Bible study, which left me grateful for all I'd learned. I took advantage of my children being away at school to clean my home. As I dusted and vacuumed, two concepts from the Bible study surfaced—to allow God complete control of my life and to be content with the path that he had set before me.

I prayed during this mid-morning cleaning frenzy, thanking God for his faithfulness to me during my unfaithfulness to him. I recall telling him I was ready to follow whatever plans he had for me, saying, "Use me as you will."

The same moment I prayed, a surprising inner voice hurled out the following words to God, "Just don't touch my kids." Embarrassed that I uttered such a request and with such force, I even blushed. I quickly re-worded my request to a more acceptable form, "Please, protect my children from harm, and keep them well."

A mere two months after "the prayer," my six-year-old son Jack was diagnosed with a brain tumor the size of a baseball. During the next four years, as my son fought for his life, I fought for my relationship with God.

I remembered the prayer I had spoken a couple of months earlier and realized that the Holy Spirit had revealed to me my deepest fear—God's precious way to clearly define my weakness. I found myself wanting to hold my children closer to my heart than even my relationship with God himself.

That day when I woke up and all was well, did I realize my weakness? No. But, over the course of the following four years, I would hold on to God with the strongest grip I could. I knew he would not leave or forsake me, but I wasn't so sure I wouldn't leave or forsake him. I had done it before.

The woman who had felt so content with life and God had wobbly legs. I wanted to be content. I wanted to be faithful. But in order for me to have peace within me, I would have to reconcile how God could allow my little son to suffer. No easy answer arrived, but I remained true to my pursuit of God. I breathed in his words from scripture. I breathed out my cries in prayer.

My family rejoices in the present-day healing Jack has experienced, knowing God held us up each step of those difficult days of surgery, chemo, and gamma knife radiation. Through that time, God lifted me to a new place with him. Now, each day, I find peace and contentment in the life that is ours to walk.

And once again I say, "Use me as you will."

Memorize and pray these scriptures to overcome complaining.

Praise: "Praise the LORD, O my soul, and forget not all his benefits" (Ps. 103:2).
Petition: "I do believe; help me overcome my unbelief" (Mark 9:24).

As you consider the questions, remember:

- Complaining sabotages contentment.
- Grumbling among family and friends creates complaint-siblings.
- Tell God, not your companions.
- Fast from complaining.
- Train toward more trust in God.

1. "I pour out my complaint before him . . . When my spirit grows faint within me, it is you who know my way" (Ps. 142:2-3). Recall a time when you experienced a wilting of your inner person. How did you reach a better place?

2. On a scale of 1-10, with one representing a chronic complainer and ten a nomination for sainthood, how much do you complain?

3. What person most often hears your complaints? How does your complaining affect them?

4. What success have you had with godly training? What steps did you take that might help others?

5. Have you had a Jeremiah-moment when you really poured out your complaints to God, perhaps even blaming him for your troubles? How did God soften your heart toward the truth of his constant care?

6. "It Is Well with My Soul," is a familiar song echoing the Shunammite's words. If you have settled in your heart that Jesus Christ is Savior and rescuer of your soul, how do you put this into practice when troubles arrive?

7. In a day, how often do you praise or bless God? If you don't know, try counting.

8. Word a simple prayer praising God for his goodness and ask that he perfect you to do "all things without murmuring or complaining."

Chapter Four

WORRISOME WAYS

Wipe out Fretting

Do not be anxious about anything . . . .

Philippians 4:6

When I told a friend in his early eighties that I had gained three pounds, he said, "That's worrisome." That word "worrisome" fits so many situations—it defines the problem of worry from the Garden of Eden until our present time. Years ago, Jesus addressed the topic of worry, yet worry still tempts us today. The habit of chronic worry can severely cripple contentment and our spheres of influence for the gospel.

Worry and Its Offspring

When compiling chapters, I pondered which of these two most endangers contentment—complaining or worry. Finally, I came to the conclusion that they are comparable in their destruction. It simply depends upon which one is most worrisome to us. To one person, complaining may be the harsh habit that wears down their faith. Another person may harbor so many worries that anxious thoughts crowd out basic truths about God our Father, the real abiding place.

Worry is a temptation that pops up every day. And we either succumb to hand wringing or give our troubling thoughts or circumstances to God.

Worry can cause real agony and, eventually, develop into a form of self torture. We become sleep deprived. Illnesses may overtake us. Gloomy countenances mask joint-heirs-with-Christ reality.

Worry also compels us to make up mental "what if" lists. What if I lose my job? What if my paycheck is cut? What if my husband won't forgive me? What if the cancer returns? What if the economy goes into another slump?

Some folk deal with worry in other destructive ways. They run to a bag of Oreos. They drink alcohol to reach a mind-numbing state. They "shop 'til they drop." They binge on TV. They sleep excessively. They run out of patience. They yell.

We even apply the phrase "I'm worried sick" when we wrangle with problems because constant worry can endanger our physical condition. Health experts and our own experiences have proven that worry and overthinking problems can cause negative effects on body, mind, and spirit.

But how do we downsize worry? How do we learn godly contentment? How can we train ourselves not to be anxious about "anything"? If you worry—from a little to a lot—read how a simple dinner fork can remind you to turn control over to God.

Dinner Forks and Living in the Current Moment

One day when I was extremely tired and hand washing a few dishes, I thought about how many times a single dinner fork might be washed over the lifetime of a household. As I multiplied years and tallied numbers, I grew overwhelmed.

Assume that you'll live in your home fifty years. You will wash a single dinner fork nearly forty-two thousand times. And that total subtracts the utensil-free meals of sandwiches and fast food. Washing that one dinner fork makes up only one small detail of my future life. Can you imagine how much I could worry over the future if I walk into the laundry room and start numbering how many times socks and underwear will be washed, folded, and put away?

That day at my kitchen sink, God's truth reached me when I recalled Jesus' reassuring words, "[D]o not worry about your life" (Matt. 6:25). God is fully aware of how our minds travel into future days, way ahead of our bodies living in real time. With my hands still sudsy in the dish water, it really hit me how many times I worry into the future over a myriad of "what-ifs." Is it any wonder that Jesus longs for us to rest in the individual moments of life and not worry about the future?

My hazy what-ifs and guesses about the future are not valid. I can conjure up all sorts of scenarios—minor to major, positive or negative—that might happen in the days ahead, but they don't influence the outcome of tomorrow. That night at the sink, I first allowed myself to grow weary of washing future dinner forks instead of issuing thanks for dinnerware, food, and a husband and two children to feed.

Jesus said to live in the here and now, the moment you are breathing in. Don't worry about tomorrow-fragments. He knows our lives are filled with minute details of work and relationships. He longs for us to be free from worries so that we can see and help the needy around us. He knows that tomorrow has enough dinner forks of its own. Throughout our lifetimes, when we selfishly worry into months ahead or bemoan the past, we overlook blessed opportunities to sacrifice praise. When we de-program worry, we become more in tune with others' needs, and we can act with wisdom. "Be wise in the way you act toward outsiders; make the most of every opportunity . . . . so that you may know how to answer everyone" (Col. 4:5-6).

If you are a worrier, a fork-reminder can help. Tape a piece of paper around the handle of a fork with Jesus' words: "Do not worry about your life." Be creative and place the fork in an out-of-the-ordinary place, the bathroom counter top, the garage work bench, the cup holder in your car (tines pointed down), or your underwear drawer.

My fork sits at my computer desk, reminding me to appreciate current blessings. My hope rests in these facts:

- Jesus understands how minds wander into the future and past.
- Jesus gifts us with small increments of time.
- Jesus knows that I can only handle minutes at a time.

Giving up Worry and Living in the Moment

Worrisome thoughts have less of a chance of overtaking us if we dwell in the current moment, because God's grace dwells in that timeframe. That's a very good reason not to live in yesterday or tomorrow. God's presence covered the past and God will walk us through the future, but we do not live in the past or future. We live in the present. As we take in each breath, that is where we live—moment by moment.

Why do folk tend to dwell in the past? Those days cannot be relived. Regrettable things in the past cannot be undone. We have hope that God can redeem them or use them to some good as he did when Joseph's brothers sold him into slavery. Joseph—elevated to a prominent government position—furnished Egypt's food supply to save his family from starvation. Or David—who rebelled against God and committed adultery—made a U-turn and became a billboard of restoration for many later generations.

Or some folk long for the "good old days," through rose-colored glasses recalling greener yesteryear pastures. They miss the days of porches and neighbors waving hello, but they forget the hot nights without air conditioning and that people rarely bought deodorant.

And why focus so much time, effort, and energy on what might happen tomorrow? Worry is pointless. Worry is draining. I find the greatest contentment when I am not bemoaning the past or hand-wringing over the future.

I am most content when I am *fully* aware of the moment I'm living. God is near, a steady help in both calm and dangerous moments. God abides with each of us, "an ever present help in trouble" (Ps. 46:1).

The only moment any of us can change or affect is the one we're breathing in right now, the one where God's mercy is active. That causes a shout of joy! At this minute, while you read, you have blessed assurance of

God's wisdom and presence. Your greatest power in Christ abides in this very moment.

When that fact nestles down into our hearts and souls, it brings contentment—a place where the joy of God can abide and flourish. When God reigns in lives, that peace and joy of the Lord attracts those burdened by the worries of this world.

Jesus showed us how to totally embrace life one breath at a time, fully obeying God in each moment. I believe that's how he evaded worry—because of his full fellowship with our Father. Jesus knew that his future fit perfectly into God's plan. These classic words uttered by Jesus bookend his life: "I have come to do your will, O God" (Heb. 10:7); and when he finished his work, he said with confidence, "Father, into your hands I commit my spirit" (Luke 23:46).

Most of us prepare some kind of list at the start of our week—a grocery list, a to-do list, or a list of errands. Besides the dinner fork and scripture, another way I remind myself to quit worrying and live in the moment, is to write "JESUS" in bold color at the top of each of my lists. His name at the top prompts me to follow in his trail of minute-by-minute sacrifices to God. I'm reminded daily that his whole life embodied grace and truth, one day at time, and he ably accomplished in thirty-three years what our Father planned for him to do.

Rebuking the Spirit of Worry

I've heard some say they rebuke Satan when worries take over, worries that block out contentment. They may say, "Get behind me, Satan," or "I rebuke you in the name of Jesus." They intone these rebukes after so many things go wrong in a day they recognize that a devil lurks behind the mischief.

It has taken awhile for me to come to this conclusion (I'm a slow learner, a remedial Christian who has to repeat classes), but I've decided not to get into a conversation with Satan ever again. I had rather turn to God. "Do not be anxious about anything, but in everything, by prayer and petition, with thanksgiving, present your requests to God" (Phil. 4:6). So when a spirit of worry tempts me, I have learned to ask God's help rather than to word-tussle with the devil.

I turn the battle with evil over to God for three reasons. First, God alone is the match for Satan. Not me. When Eve listened and responded to Satan she got into big trouble. A conversation with the devil is no minor occurrence. The New Testament writer Jude relates a historical moment when he says Archangel Michael "did not dare to bring a slanderous accusation against [the devil], but said, 'The Lord rebuke you!'" (v. 9).

Second, God's word shields his followers. When tempted, Jesus quoted God's word to ward off Satan. Armed with power-imbued scripture, Jesus-in-the-flesh deflected three fiery temptations Satan had rigged to snare him and spoil our salvation. God's living and active word remains "[s]harper than any double-edged sword, it penetrates even to dividing soul and spirit, joints and marrow; it judges the thoughts and attitudes of the heart" (Heb. 4:12).

Third, God's words also judge the thoughts of Satan's heart. God's word remains far superior to my rebukes or grappling. When any temptation or worry arrives, go directly to God and ask him to erect a protective shield around you. Jesus had glorious results, which we can also expect to receive:

- The devil left him.
- Angels arrived to minister.
- Power and authority infused his ministry.

Marthas among Us

Worry over everyday things may be the most common of all our troublesome thoughts. Without exploring all the scriptures about the prominent New Testament sisters Mary and Martha, let's think about the scene in

Martha's home (Luke 10:38-42). At a women's day event, Betty McDaniel said that sometimes she is "Martha-to-the-bone." Me, too! Do you find yourself—like Martha—worrying about the meaningless while passing over the worthwhile?

Jesus and his disciples arrived in Bethany where Martha invited them to refresh themselves in her home. I reveal Martha-like tendencies when I invite people over and then, YIKES! The numerous details of making folk comfortable assail me. After all, I have hostessing standards!

I love that it was Martha who initiated an invitation to the dusty travelers—Jesus, his disciples, and maybe other men and women in his entourage. Readers unduly judge Martha sometimes. Through this occasion as hostess, she becomes labeled as a worrier. But remember, she had the heart of a hostess and opened her home to the traveling Lord and his weary disciples.

To serve refreshments or even a light meal to a dozen or more would have been no small task. Imagine the labor-intensive preparations involved with getting food from the market to table, plucking a chicken and tucking it into a stewpot. She certainly didn't get any help from Mary. No wonder Martha felt overwhelmed! At some point during the flurry of that day, Mary "sat at the Lord's feet listening to what he said." Miffed, Martha approached Jesus: "Lord, don't you care that my sister has left me to do the work all by myself? Tell her to help me!" (Luke 10:40).

Picture the scene at Martha's house where an intimate group of friends gather: Very much at ease with one another, they undoubtedly show their emotions—Martha toward Jesus and Jesus toward Martha. In the recorded conversations of our Lord with others, he sometimes repeated the name of the person addressed ("Simon, Simon," "Saul, Saul"). I imagine Jesus' facial expression as understanding, with a good dose of warmth in his voice, as he said to his hostess, "Martha, Martha, you are worried and upset about many things, but only one thing is needed" (v. 41). Though Martha's words revealed her discontent, our insightful Lord guided her away from her worries.

After Jesus' gentle rebuke, perhaps Martha surveyed the spread of dumplings, fruit, bread, and cheese. I can just imagine her—hands on hips—saying, "You're right, Lord. It is enough." Maybe she turned to the disciples and said, "Brothers, sisters, enjoy. Help yourselves." I see her joining her sister Mary, grabbing her hand, and then pleading with her eyes for Mary's and Jesus' forgiveness. She could have. Dr. Luke doesn't share the rest of the story with us.

The Pulpit Commentary refers to Martha's anxiety as a "petulant outburst of jealousy in the living, busy matron." Who among us hasn't had a breakdown of that sort? A "temporary petulance."[1] Loosely translated, that means a short-term tantrum. Such petty things that cause them— they're what I stumble over nearly every day.

In this world, there are "Marys," those who are more contemplative, and there are "Marthas," those who do the day-to-day chores. Even in homes and workplaces today, many people work behind the scenes to enable preachers, thinkers, speakers, and writers to go on with their work. "Your Marys could not sit at Jesus' feet unless the Marthas were going about the house."[2] A hearty hooray for the keepers of our homes! We should note that Jesus did not disparage homemaking, but only Martha's tendency toward allowing the tasks to become a burden.

I've no doubt that Martha often had Mary's help in the kitchen, but on the day of Jesus' visit, cooking, cleaning and serving held no allure for Mary. She had a deeper yearning. *The Transforming Word* commentary says Mary's choice counters "prevailing expectations of women in first century culture."[3] Their roles were of a domestic nature which often included self-denial. Jesus' words about Mary, that she had "chosen what is better," affirmed that God saw women as not only domestics but disciples as well.

Mary smelled all the good food aromas that day. She was aware of feet and dishes to be washed, but the one good thing of lasting value was Jesus Christ, truth in person. Mary made a bold choice. She defied the conventional service of a woman. She grabbed hold of a rare opportunity.

On that day, both Jesus and Martha offered bread. Martha's bread would soon be forgotten. No one on earth can tell you what meal she prepared. No one can name a single recipe or spice she used, but Jesus' everlasting bread is still with us.

We can learn contentment whether we are a Mary-Martha mix or we lean toward being a doer such as Martha or a contemplative like Mary. Both are welcome in the kingdom. Both are needed. When the to-do list requires the baking of bread, the cleaning of a house, then work the chores with joy and without fretting. When a day offers time with Jesus who feeds souls, choose to quiet your Martha and abide in a Mary-moment with Jesus.

- Do-er or listener?
- Busy or quiet?
- Bread of earth?
- Bread of heaven?
- Choose well.

Worries beyond Our Thresholds

"Sweep around your own doorsteps before you sweep around your neighbor's." That southern idiom teaches us to look at our own faults rather than judging others'. That same idea can encompass *where* our worries roam. With the influx of world news, it's easy to fret over troubles thousands of miles from our back doors: natural disasters we cannot undo, massive suffering we have no means to alleviate, or war-torn areas of generational hostilities.

Absorbing a constant stream of bad news affects our contentment. Of course, empathy for human tragedy separates us from the beasts of the field, but we sometimes ingest world messes that were never meant to be ours. They rest in God's providence.

If we are called to relieve the hunger of a child or lift a burden ten thousand miles away, then we need to act. If we can assist in building tent cities to shelter refugees, then we should. If we are called to contribute funds to drill a well in a desert village instead of installing a swimming pool in our backyard, we need to do that. And sometimes we have no means to do any of the above and we rely on our compassionate God to intervene and relieve the suffering.

The bottom line is, God calls us to action and prayer but not to worldwide worry. To worry over things beyond our help is to meddle in God's realm, and meddling undermines contentment.

Worry wanders. It can roam worldwide or it can meander down the street. Instead of worrying about things beyond God's intended work for us, lay concerns at the feet of miracle-worker God. He is powerful enough to take care of his creation. God houses a compassionate heart and has a bread-of-earth storehouse of manna, quail, milk and honey, and net-breaking catches of fish.

Other earthly horrors can cause worry, too. The wicked perpetrate evil against innocents that makes us physically sick to our stomachs: war crimes, the sexual abuse of a child, or spousal assault. Or innocent Amish schoolgirls are shot, killing five and maiming others for life. What about the acts perpetrated on September 11, 2001? Evil abounds. Evil that we can't control. Evil we can't explain. Evil that God knows is going on. Evil that God will someday totally alleviate.

While I abhor wickedness, I also know that God can act far beyond my futile worry about such events. During horrible happenings in the world or in our communities, we can find rest. We may not sleep well for a few nights—such is the disturbance of unsettling news—but rest from worry can come because we trust that God is not blind to the suffering of the innocents and he knows how to rescue and relieve.

While I regret bringing worry and other pitiable sins to God, by faith I sense his forgiveness even as I lay them at his feet. He teaches me. He mends. He heals. He restores. He will transform our scattered, worried minds. He will help us learn contentment even in the chaos of this world as we remember:

- Worry wanders.
- God watches over me.
- God watches over his world.

Adding Hours to Life

Jesus offered this thought-provoking question: "Who of you by worrying can add a single hour to your life?" (Matt. 6:27). In reality we lose hours upon hours when we worry—hours that could be productive if we spent them caring for family, sitting at his feet, reading to our babies, sharing the gospel, or helping aging parents. Worry diminishes our hours when we could be working to make a difference. When we defeat worry—with God's help and implemented prayer—we add hours, days, or even years to our lives.

When King Hezekiah knew that death was imminent, he prayed to the Lord to intervene and God honored his request. The Lord added an additional fifteen years to his life (2 Kings 20:1-11). That excites me. For King Hezekiah, a breathless chasm existed between worry-about-dying and a prayer for restored health.

Worry can become so ingrained, so much a habitual part of our being that we fail to recognize when our thoughts travel down those paths. When we hear sirens, we may conjure an image of an injured loved one, and before we know it, our thoughts have not served us but have betrayed us. Wasted thoughts. Wasted emotions. Wasted minutes—minutes we could have prayed for the real person who suffered trauma.

Trouble taints all our lives. To alleviate worry, practice your faith—trust God and his timing. My mother has lain in a hospital bed for over three years in an irreversible, painfully slow physical decline. I have no power to heal or halt her illness. I cannot hasten her eternal relief. I confess I often wonder why the Lord has delayed in rescuing her. And then one day as I leaned over and combed her hair, she came out of her dementia long enough to gently tap me over my heart and deliver a word from the Lord:

"He has promised to do us good not evil all the days of our lives." Oh, how I needed her sweet reminder. Even in her suffering, my mother led me away from worry to contentment when she pointed me toward God.

During the reading of this chapter and meditating on scripture, you may have recognized deep-seated habits of worry. If so, I challenge you to track your worries for one day. When a worry surfaces, write down one or two words identifying it. At the end of the day, look over your list. Are there any circumstances which could be changed by worrying about them? Learning to recognize the temptation to worry is a first step to recovering a prayerful spirit instead of a fretful one.

꒰ ⟨ ⟩ ꒱

Embracing Contentment
Joan Clayton's Story

"Ouch! Stop it! That hurts!"

"Your mother sent you to visit me, and she would want you to comb your hair while you're here!" Aunt Floy, my mother's bossy sister and a "take charge" person, picked up the brush and attacked me like a lawn mower. "Do you go to first grade looking like that?"

"You're pulling my hair out," I wailed, but Aunt Floy seemed determined to fulfill her mission. Because I'd never known such torture, I decided she didn't like me.

"Don't eat anymore ice cream," she said on my thirteenth birthday. "You're already too pudgy."

At sixteen she told me, "If you eat today, your stomach will stick out tonight in your prom dress." I starved all day. I wanted to look pretty in that beautiful, ruffled ensemble, especially since the most handsome boy in the senior class had asked me.

Years later, I married that handsome prince. In time, we had three lively sons. Aunt Floy's advice—annoying when I was younger—now stirred up my patience, as I reared my own children. Childless, she had taught school for forty-one years, which, according to her, gave her all the answers in child rearing. I endured her critical comments.

Even so, since Aunt Floy and Uncle Fred were our last living relatives, I couldn't stand the thought of their being alone at Christmas.

So they celebrated the holidays with us. As usual, Aunt Floy voiced her opinion: "My word, if I spent this much money on toys, I couldn't sleep at night! These boys didn't need all of this. How much did you spend anyway? I haven't bought a new dress in thirty years, and I'm proud of it."

Our boys and my husband, Emmitt, ignored her outbursts. "That's just her way." Emmitt tried to console me, but I berated myself for making such a poor decision. *Why did I feel sorry for her and invite them? She despises me. She didn't like me as a child, and she sure doesn't like me as an adult.* I prayed, "Lord, it's so hard for me to forgive her."

"You have to accept her as she is," Emmitt told me. His admonition hurt because I hadn't realized I still harbored bitterness. Thankfully, time passed, and I worked at overlooking offenses.

Then, one night, Uncle Fred died suddenly of a heart attack, leaving Aunt Floy all alone at eighty. "Come stay with us for a while," we pleaded.

"No! I will stay in my own home, and I don't want you to stay with me either."

One day she called Emmitt to check on her car. "It just won't start," she said in her usually grumpy voice.

"Why don't you call us when you need to go somewhere. That way you won't have to worry about your car not starting."

Emmitt came home after visiting Aunt Floy, his face troubled. "We need to allow her independence as long as we can." He took me in his arms, desperate for me not to worry.

We checked on her one evening and found her in her kitchen mixing cornstarch, cinnamon, and water in a flower vase. "I was just about to eat supper," she said. She looked so pitiable mixing that dreadful concoction for a meal standing at the cabinet in her dingy gown.

"It's time," Emmitt said to me later. Sadness overcame me as I realized we faced a challenging decision.

We investigated many nursing homes. After several days we finally found one we liked more than the others and made the arrangements. The night before we were supposed to take Aunt Floy to her new home, I said to Emmitt, "This will be the last night she will ever spend in her own home. I guess there's a last time for everything."

"She might actually be happy there," he said. Because of her sour disposition that thought had never occurred to me. I took comfort in his statement.

"Where are we going?" Aunt Floy asked early the next morning, as we helped her into the car.

"We're going to visit a lady who wants to show you a nice home." The director met us at the door and took Aunt Floy by the hand. "Let me show you a pretty room that is just for you."

"What a nice place," I heard my aunt say. Before they turned the corner, Aunt Floy stopped and looked back at me. Her eyes met mine with a sense of relief. Could that be gratitude?

The next morning we went back to the nursing home to check on her. "She's in the beauty shop," the nurse told us. "She's been busy making new friends."

I hurried down the hall and peeked in the beauty shop. Aunt Floy had been bathed and dressed in brown pants and a matching blouse.

"Hi!" She greeted me enthusiastically as she took my hand. "Come to my room. I want to show you all the clothes they gave me." I didn't try to explain I'd brought the clothes. "You'll love my room. They're nice to me here, and it doesn't cost a penny." I didn't try to explain that either.

"Thank you, Lord," I whispered. "She's happy here."

"You must be Joan," a smiling nurse said as she approached us. "Your aunt told us all about you. She must love you very much!"

I breathed a big sigh of relief. The contentment I felt at that moment filled my heart. "Thank you, Lord. Thank you for the miracle for both of us."

I finally understood. She had loved me all along!

Memorize and pray these scriptures to guard against fretting.

Praise: "He has delivered my soul in peace from the battle that was against me: for there were many with me" (Ps. 55:18 KJV).
Petition: "My thoughts trouble me and I am distraught because of what my enemy is saying" (Ps. 55:2-3).

As you consider the questions, remember:

- Worry produces bad fruit.
- Worry over the past and future is futile.
- Abide in the current moment and experience God's grace.
- Let God rebuke worrisome spirits.
- Entrust all concerns to God, who meets all needs.

1. Write down your anxious thoughts for one full day, and then ask God to purify you from "everything that contaminates body and spirit, perfecting holiness out of reverence for God" (2 Cor. 7:1).

2. Looking back, can you remember a time when you experienced a physical illness due to worry? Have you known someone who was "worried sick?" How did the worry affect you or them?

3. What everyday things in life are you most tempted to worry about? What are your current minor problems? Do you have larger worrisome things afflicting your life?

4. The opposite of worry is deep abiding joy and trust in the Lord. God is our strength, and our song, and the joy of our salvation (Ps. 118:14; 51:12). On a scale of 1-10, what is your joy quotient? Is worry hampering your joy?

5. Read Acts 16:19-25. Paul and Silas suffered severe beatings, a dark jail cell, and shackles around their ankles for the cause of Christ. At midnight—after a tougher-than-tough day—they prayed and sang

hymns. How does their reaction compare to the way you typically respond to even lesser trials?

6. The Acts 16 text says the other prisoners listened to Paul and Silas. Through our contentment we bear witness to the peace of God that passes all understanding (Phil. 4:7). People listen. People watch. Has someone noticed your peace or joy and inquired about its source?

7. Fill in the blanks. Have you sought the Lord with a similar complaint to Martha's: "Lord, don't you care that_____has left me to do the work all by myself?" If the Lord had answered back like he did to Martha, would his reply fit you? "_____,_____, you are worried and upset about _____, but only one thing is needed."

8. Write a simple prayer praising God for the song of joy you can "sing" to the world. List your worries, and then ask him to restore the hours you waste on worry and instead use those hours to his glory.

Chapter Five

PERMIT LOADS
The Balanced Life

Teach us to number our days aright, that we may gain a heart of wisdom.

Psalm 90:12

One Tuesday morning I ran behind schedule. I hurriedly tidied the family room, got the kids off to school, and gathered notes for the women's Bible class lesson I would teach. When hunger pangs hit, I dashed to the kitchen and grabbed a couple of peanut butter crackers. With only minutes to finish getting ready, I rushed to the shower, hopped in, and started to wash my face. Imagine my surprise when I found a half-eaten cracker protruding from my mouth.

I laughed aloud at the absurdity of the moment, and said to myself, "When you eat 'breakfast' in the shower . . . you're too busy!" That became a pivotal moment for me. I longed to avoid overbooking my schedule again.

I wish I could tell you that over-crowding my days never occurred after that, but it did. I wish I could say I'd learned my lesson so strongly I never again rushed crazily from one event to the next, but I can't. As life moves forward it fluctuates and causes an ongoing need to reassess, prioritize, and pare down again and again. In this chapter we'll consider a major stumbling block to contentment—overcrowding life.

Heavy Loads

Federal and state highway departments have strict rules about the weight and width of cargo placed on trucks and trailers. When trucks bear "Oversized Load" signs, those signify that state officials have pre-routed them over the strongest bridges and under overpasses with plenty of clearance. The state also limits their travel hours. Usually, smaller trucks with flashing yellow lights escort them. You've probably encountered these specially permitted cargos on your travels, and you know to give these big and cumbersome loads a wide passageway.

We have sensible laws that govern highways because overloaded trucks and trailers can damage our nation's infrastructure or cause hazards for fellow travelers. When it comes to our personal loads, adults self-govern (or they should!), and although we may realize we are overbooked, some are reluctant or lackadaisical about stopping their fleets, removing weight, and making much-needed changes.

Some overloading develops from the outskirts of lives—because we know so many people and own lots of possessions. As we move forward in years, it is wise to trim our life-attachments. Compare an overbooked life to a six-year-old child who still wears clothing from when he was four. Shirts threaten to pop buttons. Trousers become high water pants. And his undergarments put things in a bind. As more time passes in life, we add more people and possessions. Adjustments must be made. We "do" life better when we reassess and re-outfit every few years—seams don't rip and cause a spectacle.

Think with me for a moment about how quickly we make additions to life. From the time we're born until gray hairs sprout from scalps, new people come into our lives. We gain a family with our birth certificate. Later, if we marry, we gain another family unit. Then children may come along through birth, adoption, or foster care, and in those years, we meet many people through our children's activities. We may be outfitted with all of this even before we reach the age of thirty.

Throughout our adult lives, we continue to meet people through church, work, school, clubs, and neighborhoods. We share milestone events with them. We even get to meet their network of friends at various events, including births, weddings, graduations, retirements, and funerals.

Through social networks such as Facebook and Twitter, we can expand our connections ever further. Not too long ago, an author asked me to become her Facebook friend, but when I accepted her invitation the system turned me down. She already had five thousand friends!

We interact with more people than fifty years ago, because we no longer need to meet face-to-face to conduct business. Through a Christian Writers' internet forum, I met five delightful, Spirit-filled women, all fellow newspaper columnists, who helped pray me through the writing of my first book, and then became my co-authors on another book. We're spread across Ohio, Texas, and California, and before we co-authored, *A Scrapbook of Christmas Firsts*, most of us had never met in person.

As you can see, we have the potential to rub physical or virtual shoulders with thousands of people during our lives. In addition, other things, such as possessions and passions, can fill up a lifetime.

Our possessions can cause overload. Imagine a giant Radio Flyer wagon containing all your stuff—outdoor equipment, household items, junk drawer trinkets, clothing, etc. Too much cargo can result in axle damage and cause the frame of your wagon to tilt. If you continue to add cargo but rarely unload any of it, the whole load can become unbalanced and you risk collapsing. (Check out the next chapter, "Bedazzled," for a more thorough examination of our collections of stuff.)

We must include our passions in the list of things that chew up hours of our lives—things like art, music, volunteering, sports, reading, studying, designing, exercising, building, or media entertainment. In some cases, these refresh our spirits. But if these extracurricular activities fill too many timeslots, they can cause mental stress and snatch great chunks of time from schedules instead of renewing us as they were originally intended to do.

I'm living proof that, before you know it, you will celebrate many birthdays. While I don't regret meeting any of the people I have along the way—well, most of them—I often wonder how I accumulated so much stuff! As I review my years, I regret time wasted on unworthy endeavors. But I can point to other things I know were right choices. For example, I'm not apologetic for any nap I *ever* took. My niece kept trying to phone us on weekend afternoons. When she shared with me her lack of success, I came clean with her, "Honey, weekend afternoons are reserved for naps."

Young and energetic, she laughed, "Y'all are nap-taking fools." She has me pegged.

If you decide to whittle your schedule, don't cut sleep or rest time to the bare bones. Like toddlers, we're all much more pleasant when we get our naps with our blankies.

You've heard the adage "Time flies." I concur. Calendar pages flip at an alarming rate these days. When I was younger, I rushed the years. When will I get my driver's license? When will I have a home of my own? When will these toddlers be able to get a drink by themselves? When will the kids finish college? Then, one year, I noticed how quickly spring, summer, autumn, and winter passed, and my questions screeched to a halt.

Recognizing and living out the seasons of life to their fullness will help us maintain a balance that supplements contentment. We won't wish away the days or long for a languid future. Instead, with God as instructor, we'll learn to "number our days aright, that we may gain a heart of wisdom" (Ps. 90:12).

Spring, Summer, Autumn, and Winter

God set in motion earth's yearly seasons—birth, renewal, clean up, and rest. He mirrors the seasons of earth in his crowning work—mankind. If we want to travel through life with a balanced load, recognize the ways God's natural world reflects our youth, mid-life, and later years. Doing so gives us a distinct advantage: Contentment will more readily accompany life's stages. Consider the changes at each season of life.

The time from birth to youth resembles springtime. Babies don't own much, but by the time they reach their teenage years, they've amassed a whole passel of items. A toddler doesn't know very many people, but most teenagers collect friends like they collect phone numbers—a bunch of them.

An individual's summer season represents a time of reproduction, blooming, and vitality. This season includes education, wedding bells, and home building. And we add more acquaintances and a lot of household items as our families grow.

By life's autumn, a person's energy lessens. Some people have gained weight, lost hair, and collected a facial palette of wrinkles. Depending upon how often we purge possessions—our earthly goods can fill any space from a small cottage to a six thousand square foot house, with little space left. Picture narrow carpet trails between stacks of stuff as you try to walk from room to room. And don't forget those full storage units in the back yard or off site!

Winter means winterizing—preparing for the inevitable moment when we will step beyond this world. In this last season, the sap has slowed dramatically. A former matriarch, who once effortlessly hosted the entire family, may need caretakers to help with minor things like finding reading glasses and remembering appointments. She may also need help with everyday tasks, such as eating, bathing, clothing, and taking medications. In all likelihood, someone will take away her car keys.

I suspect that a senior-citizen psalmist wrote these words: "Lord, you gave me only a short life. My short life is nothing, compared to you. Every person's life is only like a cloud (that quickly disappears). No person lives forever" (39:5 ERV).

But even in these years of reduced physical strength, it's possible for our faith to peak. Our greatest faith tasks may lie ahead just as they did for Moses and Abraham. Moses began to lead Israel at eighty. Abraham was well over a hundred when God arranged a faith showdown like no other—to sacrifice his and Sarah's only son.

Ultimately, it's critical that we stop our rolling wagons from time to time—spring, summer, fall, and winter—and revisit God's dreams and hopes for our lives. Take an honest look at schedules and possessions. Take inventory.

You may need to designate certain days each year to catalog possessions. Open the door to the junk room or garage and imagine the useable space if it were cleared of just the outdated and broken things. Assess the items in and around your home, tally the outdoor and sports equipment, the dishes, the sweaters, and the electronic gadgets. What do you actually use? What only takes up space? Pray that God will guide you to an honest assessment and the will to let go of non-beneficial items.

- Stop the wagon.
- Weigh the cargo.
- Get rid of the unnecessary.
- Move on.

Unload Little Red Wagons

Not only do adults need to watch overloading, some kids have far too much in their Radio Flyers. And since they don't drive themselves to drama practice, soccer, and equestrian lessons, parents get caught up in children's over-scheduling as they chauffeur in SUVs and minivans.

Parents, discuss ground rules for rearing children. If you frequently repeat family rules to your child when they are young, you'll have fewer whine fests along the way. Your children will know what your family expects.

Our family's first rule was to prioritize corporate worship. Gathering with fellow believers to honor God came before other activities. This rule guided our family, although we made a few exceptions along the way.

Our kids participated in the youth activities at church and they were allowed involvement in one outside activity at a time. One activity—baseball or Cub Scouts, band or choir, guitar lessons or football. We consistently enforced this effort to keep them from over-scheduling, which could lead to frustrations and meltdowns.

Some parents enroll kids in too many play activities when their children could learn comparative skills or even more worthy skills at home while interacting with siblings and parents. I often repeat this mantra to young moms, "Teach them to work. They know how to play."

Parents sometimes drift along instead of making a conscious effort to train their children in godliness and to teach them life- and work-skills in the home. I see couples and single parents exhausted from chauffeuring kids to soccer, dance, swim team, and baseball. Make time to live out—in your home and on the go—Spirit inspired "love, joy, peace, patience, kindness, goodness, faithfulness, gentleness and self-control" (Gal. 5:22).

Do you often find yourself hurrying to the next event? Does your week rush by to the point where your good intentions of instructing your children about God get laid aside? God intended that parents be his primary representatives to little ones—not Sunday schools, mentors, or spiritual DVDs. Protect the sanctity of family time, or you may find your family doing a lot of things—and none of them well.

- Make time to listen—to hear what your child's heart really longs for.
- Make time to attract your child to want more of God not gadgets.
- Make time to visit the sick with your child, not just visit the ballpark.
- Make time with your child to explain and explore God.

Early on, some families train their children to go, go, go. But, in that situation, when do children get opportunities to develop Christ-like disciplines of solitude and silence? Do we set a pace for peace? How do we encourage them to be happy travelers when their loads are too heavy? Do you have contented children? Remember, children learn contentment—from parents and God. God is content. Are you? Ask yourself and then give yourself an honest answer, "Do I have contented children or just busy children?"

Meals at the Family Table

I love memories of our young family. Dinner time at the table. Bath time. Bedtime. We found early mornings to be the best time for longer discussions about God. Before school, we spent extra time at the breakfast table reading through stories in the Old Testament (I paraphrased many of these). When our oldest child Russell turned eleven, we began concentrating more on the life of Jesus while they crunched on their Cheerios and syrup-ed their pancakes.

If families overbook their schedules, they have a tendency to miss those mealtimes around their family table. The National Center on Addiction and Substance Abuse (CASA) at Columbia University found many positives for the family who eats meals together. After ten years of gathering data, researchers found that families who rarely eat together have less healthy meals, meager conversation, and children who lack motivation for learning.

CASA discovered that families who eat together fewer than three times a week often have the television on during mealtimes, and after questioning the children in these families, researchers determined that they are much less likely to say their parents are proud of them. As children move into the teen years, research shows that they need this crucial hour at the table with family, but they are less likely to get it because of hectic schedules. Because both parents work and children have after school activities, some families blow in the door of their homes somewhere near bedtime and enjoy very little interaction with each other—or none at all.

This research also shows that teens who don't bring their electronic devices to the dinner table and who have their parent's attention at five to seven family meals a week are less likely to smoke, use drugs, or drink alcohol. They are also more likely to achieve As and Bs in school, rather than Cs and lower. Their food choices are healthier and they learn to eat a variety of foods rather than have a "food court mentality:" Mom wants a burrito, Dad prefers Chinese, and the teen orders a shake and fries.[1]

The choices you make for your family will affect their relationship to God and to you. God is your source for guidance, and James tells us: "If any of you lacks wisdom, he should ask God, who gives generously to all without finding fault, and it will be given to him" (1:5). Parents and grand-parents, make praying for wisdom a priority as you mentor your families.

Does your family need to slow down, unload? Get ready. Get set. Go—but gear your family down to a slower speed. Don't overload them at any age—from two to eighteen. Don't be a part of putting your kids on the fast track. The family track is yours. Make it work in favor of God by providing a framework where they can learn contentment.

- Limit children's activities.
- Children benefit from free-play and work at home.
- Gather your family around the table.
- Pray for wisdom.

Are Family Activities Covered by Prayer?

"And pray in the Spirit on all occasions with all kinds of prayers and re-quests" (Eph. 6:18). Do you wrap your individual pursuits and family ac-tivities in prayer? Are family involvements sanctioned and blessed because you prayed for guidance? Do you plan your schedules by talking to God first, before adding or subtracting? If our ordinary routines are grounded in Spirit-led prayers, then when those unexpected—good or not-so-good—things happen that require extra investments of time, we cope more readily.

So many times, a family takes in one organized event after another, when what they really need is nourishment and refreshment time in their homes—homes which have been set apart from the world by prayer.

Trish Berg, an author and national speaker (and my co-author on a holiday book) told me that one day she was a guest on a live radio show.

When a radio host and the guest live in different cities, the host phones the guest a few minutes before the program airs. This particular interview was to last one hour, from noon until 1:00 P.M. As a mom of four, Trish understands that children sometimes get fidgety when moms talk on the phone overly long. Trish was prepared. Colin—four-years-old—had eaten, and he had Crayolas, books, Play Dough, and trucks, all at hand. For the first fifty minutes of the interview, Colin remained quiet and docile, but when Trish saw Colin lie down in the floor near her feet and begin to fidget and make whining noises, she knew her little son had maxed out. Watching mom on the phone for one hour proved to be too much for a tired four-year-old.

As a last resort, to keep Colin quiet for just a few more minutes. Trish opened her kitchen freezer, frantically looking for something—anything. She grabbed a frozen bag of chocolate chips, ripped them open with her teeth, and dropped them to Colin, who was now wrapped around her ankles.

The ruse worked and Trish got through the interview while Collin happily sugar-binged on the frozen chocolate chips. Trish, a loving and attentive mom, later said she knew the long interview stretched the limits for both of them.

Families are surviving—but just barely—on the empty calories that the world offers. Families need the healthy nutrition that comes from a calm, God-nourished home. But when the world calls, too often we answer the door and join in the commotion. Building a God-fearing family isn't for sissies. It requires effort, discipline, and diligence—something we don't have when we're stretched too thin.

Promote contentment in your family by scheduling spare time in each day. That extra time can be used for the unexpected "pauses" that happen almost every day. Allow an hour or more to alter your schedule if needed.

On the plain days of life, the regular days, are you, your family, and your ministries covered in prayer? When they are set apart through prayer,

God can help you arrange family schedules so he becomes the heartbeat of your home. God remains the source to inspire courage to do this.

God cares about your schedules and your pressures. Based on many stories from the Word, God proves how he cares about even the small details of life. When God exterminated pests in Egypt, not a single fly remained. He made a lost ax head float to the top of the water so the man who borrowed it could return it.

I think the hairs on our heads have numbers because God wants to show how intimately he cares about us. Consider sparrows—more prolific than even the Israelites—not one can tumble out of its nest without God seeing and caring. God's concise knowledge of each cell in our bodies, each fear, and each snippet of our lives gives us courage to pray about small things.

Always listening, God can help us clear the chaos and replace it with contentment. However, if we neglect prayer for each of our family's involvements, we work from our weaknesses. Oh, we may get through each day—rear families, perform our jobs, attend school, and do the many extras—but the missing components are making time to train in godliness and the receiving of joy and contentment.

When those are absent, our lives become drudgery. Joy, joy, joy is down so deep it can't come up for air. Peace that could be river-sized slows down to a trickle.

How about you? Are all your family's activities covered by prayer? Do you blanket your day from beginning to end in believing prayer? Do you entrust your spouse to our Father? What about your dear children? Do you pray for your work and work place? Do you ask for grace and mercy to abide in your home, church family, and friendships?

Try spending ten minutes in the morning to list-and-lift to God your family members and their involvements for that day. This will not take much time out of your morning routine, but it will put your family in the forefront of your mind. Best of all, you have Jesus-help as you offer them and their activities into his service. Sacrifice a bit of time and utter a word of praise over them. Offer them as lights to shine as Jesus did. Your prayers will make a difference. How should you do this?

- Pray in the Spirit.
- Each morning, list and lift your family and activities.
- Make a habit of prayer-swaddling your family.

Earlier I mentioned eating "breakfast" in the shower. Afterwards, God prompted me to do a simple self test. Was my life-pace God-honoring? Did I have the presence of mind to cover mine and my family's activities in believing prayer? Or was I doing a lot of hand wringing and emergency-only prayers?

After a careful—and somewhat painful—reckoning, I came up prayer-short and heavy on the hand-wringing. God showed me that I often plowed through my days not harnessed to him. To this day, I struggle to keep my life in sync with the season, but this prompting stays with me constantly: to walk through my days with Christ's energy "which so powerfully works in me" (Col. 1:29).

Embracing Contentment
Mark Hayter's Story

Contentment is one of God's blessings hidden in plain sight. You'd think it'd be easier to find. Took me years. I kept tripping over it during my search. Imagined it somewhere in the far distance . . . at the end of the long time.

My moment of discovery occurred as I was sitting on the roof trying to come to grips with a dilemma. The roof is a good place to go for a clearer view of stuff. Been my experience.

The dilemma involved an invitation to deliver a motivational talk at an area-wide convention of Future Teachers of America. Since I had been teaching for a number of years, and since I arguably still had my wits about me, it was assumed that I might provide a wealth of positive reinforcement for prospective teachers. The logic doesn't necessarily follow, but I could see where someone might be led to assume.

Truth be known, I didn't see myself as that great of an example for anyone planning a career in education. At no time in my life had I prayed to be a teacher. It was something that just more or less happened while I was looking for something else. Something big. I had prayed for guidance in becoming a famous author, a well-known actor, a popular public speaker . . . even a Supreme Court Justice. At no time did God ever hear me mention the word "teacher" in regard to me. But that's where I ended up. Try to figure.

At first I thought teaching was just a short stop on my journey to finding "The Big Thing." After twenty years in the classroom, I was pretty sure God didn't give two hoots about The Big Thing . . . or about me. I had sought, asked, and knocked. Nothing.

So, there I was on my roof trying to come up with something to say about my quest to be a teacher—a great job, something I always wanted to do, work hard, put your mind to it . . . that kind of stuff. No way could I say, "While on the road to success, I took a weird turn and ended up being a teacher. With some serious prayer you can probably do the same." Did I mention it was a dilemma?

In the middle of my rooftop brain-wrack, I decided to do the one thing I should have done the moment I left the ladder. I bowed my head and asked God for guidance. I reminded him that he had not been all that effective in letting me accomplish something big, but maybe he could find it in his will to help with a somewhat smaller task.

After my brief prayer, I opened my eyes and gradually began to get a mental view of a younger me on Camille Street in my old neighborhood. I was running around, playing in the yard with my childhood buddies. Friends I thought would be with me always. What happened to them? Where were they? Had they been sidetracked while on their roads to success? Surely none of them were sitting on a roof trying to figure out something to say to a group of future teachers.

Then it hit me. Bonk! That was it. That was my talk. I would get up there and tell those young men and women how I came to be standing on that stage. I'd tell them the truth. Even the scary parts.

I'd tell them about my quest for The Big Thing . . . about seeking fame, fortune, and recognition. I would tell them how I tried to get God interested in my cause by explaining to him how much better it'd be for him if I were a big success. Just think of the influence for "good" I'd be if I were famous. I'd be happy, God would be happy . . . all God's children would be happy. How good is that?

But God wasn't having it. He provided no guidance. None at all. None that I could see—until I climbed to the roof. While sitting there I began to recall just a few of the hundreds of nudges God had provided me on my quest for The Big Thing. I saw the little things that he put in my path, things that made me veer a bit. Quite a bit. A whole lot.

I remembered a teacher who caused me to get off track long enough to consider a different direction. And there was a young preacher who gently urged me along the way. Acquaintances, strangers, and timely events that prompted me onto the path of becoming a school teacher.

There were the kind words from a few who graciously recommended me for positions and awards that were undeserved. Regardless, the recognition allowed me to be selected as the guest speaker for a group of young people, all wishing to be teachers.

At that moment on that roof, I saw how a myriad of life's "little things" had guided me. Each had been a part of God's plan to put me where he wanted me to be. He loved me so much that he refused to give me what I asked for. He saved me from myself by giving me his best.

Over the years, I've taught nearly four thousand students. I do not know what influence I had in the lives of any one of them. My trust and hope makes me believe that I had a small role in placing some of them on the road God meant for them to take.

My faith makes me believe that God continues to use me. That his purpose for me is in the here and now. Always has been.

That realization has made all the difference. It has allowed me to find contentment. The contentment that I should've discovered so much sooner. After all, it was right in front of me the whole time. I just kept tripping over it.

Memorize and pray these scriptures to live a more balanced life.

Praise: "Morning by morning, O Lord, you hear my voice; morning by morning I lay my requests before you and wait in expectation" (Ps. 5:3).
Petition: "Show me, O Lord, my life's end and the number of my days; let me know how fleeting is my life" (Ps. 39:4).

As you answer the questions, remember:

- Plan a balanced life for adults and children.
- If hectic, pare down schedules.
- Eat together as a family.
- Prayer-swaddle your family and all activities.

1. Count the number of people in your immediate and extended family. Also count your closest friends, coworkers, and phone buddies. Is the tally higher than you expected? How does having so many relationships impact your To Do list?

2. With life mirroring the seasons of earth, what season are you in?

3. Explain what this verse means, "Teach us to number our days aright, that we may gain a heart of wisdom" (Ps. 90:12).

4. After reading this chapter and the scriptures, has the Lord led you to recognize an overload? Can some of it be alleviated? If so, list specific ways you can accomplish that unburdening?

5. This week, try the suggestion to "list-and-lift" your family's activities to God each morning. Wait in expectation for his intervention in your days. Record results here.

_____

_____

_____

_____

_____

_____

6. When you ask for wisdom, James says God gives "generously to all without finding fault" (1:5). How will you forge that habit of asking God for wisdom?

7. Extra loads come along in life, burdens over which we have no control—illnesses, losses, accidents, or suffering because someone else sinned. How does Jesus' invitation help you? "Come to me, all you who are weary and burdened, and I will give you rest" (Matt. 11:28).

8. Word a short prayer praising God for intervention in individual lives and ask for his guidance in balancing your seasons of life.

Chapter Six

BEDAZZLED

Freedom from Overachievement and Over-Possessions

Watch out! Be on your guard against all kinds of greed;
a man's life does not consist in the abundance of his possessions.

Luke 12:15

The rhinestone, sequin, razzle-dazzle industry has exploded in recent years. All kinds of women's garments—from T-shirts to tennis shoes—sparkle with added pizzazz. People own other flashy items, too. Cell phone covers shine, shimmering notebooks hold homework assignments, and shoe-lights twinkle when children walk, skip, or hop.

Men, don't get smug about the abundance of bling on women. All the expensive extras on cars, trucks, and motorcycles put a glittered T-shirt to shame. I imagine chrome tailpipes are to a man what bejeweled shoes are to a woman.

What we used to wear to parties, we now wear to Walmart. Do you think it's possible we've topped out on sparkle? I admit, I like a nice rhinestone as well as the next girl, but glitz is wearing thin. When I cleaned out my closet, I noticed how many garments and shoes sparkled, and I questioned which shines brighter—my inside-Jesus-spirit or the glitter I wear? I'm casting my vote for more substance on the inside and less sheen on the outside. Just this week, I saw a plain T-shirt with this slogan printed across the front: "Let Your Soul Shine." Now, that's what I'm talking about!

I'd love to see the apostle Paul's face if he could stroll through a mall on a Saturday afternoon. After a blitz of glitz, perhaps he'd remind us with the Lord's words: "[L]et your light shine before men, that they may see your good deeds and praise your Father in heaven" (Matt. 5:16).

In this chapter, we'll consider two allurements which thwart contentment—overachievement and over-possessions. Both beckon with flashy, fake promises of happiness and pleasure.

Overachievement

What does overachievement mean to you? What does it look like in your life? How does it make you act? Have you ever laid aside the worthwhile to reach purely selfish goals? Symptoms of overachievement show up in abandonment of marriages, family, quiet time, and solitude. Ignoring a need for recreation and rest may be another sign of striving to have too much. Overachievement involves neglecting what's important to pursue excess.

Two family incomes are often the norm, but not every family needs their combined earned incomes to meet the necessities of life. Sometimes, we join the rat race because we want to live like the rat next door. Keeping up with the Joneses began in the Garden of Eden when Cain wanted to achieve the same status as his brother Abel. And we know where that led.

Would we be willing to live on less to invest more time in nurturing our souls? Do we really want to see a corporation succeed while our family shrivels? Does money in the bank bring the same satisfaction as God-fearing and wholesome children? What if you worded a prayer and asked God to bless the things in which you most invest your time? What would God cast his blessing upon?

Admittedly, we must spend a fair amount of time working to earn money to provide for our families. But, what drives us to want to earn more money to buy bigger—and supposedly better—stuff? Do we want better clothes, homes, cars, or possessions so we reflect success to the world? Or do we want that larger crockpot so we can feed more people and be hospitable? Do we want a new pickup with all the gizmos because we dropped by a dealership one day and the new-leather scent whisked us away to the land of loans? Or could we drive our reliable, older vehicle a few more years to further our generosity to others?

What type of statement do our earnings and ownership make to others? What do our achievements represent to God? By what standards are we guided? If the world's standards of success guide us, then success can become our god. Literary agent Chip MacGregor once shared this thought with Christians who write: "We're called to obedience, not notoriety. We're called to significance, not success."[1] His outlook could aptly fit many other occupations, too.

When our personality, our belongings, our passions, and our gifts bring glory to God—to assist in making God look good to others—that's when we can truly enjoy what God places in our domains. That's when we embrace our true calling and contentment has space to grow.

An Achievement Guideline from Wisdom Literature

Two things I ask of you, O LORD; do not refuse me before I die: Keep falsehood and lies far from me; give me neither poverty nor riches, but give me only my daily bread. Otherwise, I may have too much and disown you and say, "Who is the LORD?" Or I may become poor and steal, and so dishonor the name of my God.

(a portion of Agur's prayer, Prov. 30:7-9)

I dub this a middle-of-the-road prayer. Not many scriptures call us to mediocrity, but I believe Agur's prayer does. In this context, his request sets a standard of average achievement. He affirms that average can be a good place to reside, a place of less temptation, a place where we can still excel at our endeavors even while avoiding overachievement. With that in mind, maybe the newest T-shirt slogan for Christians could read, "Excel in Mediocrity."

Let's explore the first part of Agur's request when he asks God to erect a lie-barrier. In a twenty-four-hour day, we encounter many falsehoods. The effects of these lies cause much discontent, the opposite of tranquility. Our inner voice doesn't always speak honestly to us. We may continue to berate ourselves for a wrong after we've already been forgiven. Or conversely, after a good deed, our inner person becomes pride-filled, reminding us of how wonderful we are.

Lies from outside sources bombard us, too: mean-spirited critics sometimes speak denigrating lies to us—or about us. In a day's time, we encounter multiple deceiving messages from the world, which can cause delusions. Satan, the "father of lies" (John 8:44), lures us into wanting more of the world's goods. Through the promise of false rewards, he seduces us to entwine our fingers with the hand of darkness.

To combat deception, regularly repeat to God Agur's request, "Keep falsehood and lies far from me." This poignant request will prompt Christ-followers to stay close to the Son of God—"full of grace and truth" (John 1:14)—to repel both internal and external lies.

Let's explore Agur's second request and how it relates to overachievement. "[G]ive me neither poverty nor riches, but give me only my daily bread." Because the temptation to fill a growling stomach can override better judgment and riches can cause arrogance, Agur asks for God's help in avoiding both extremes. Of course, other temptations and resulting sins lie at either end of the spectrum—stealing and gloating are only two of them. Agur also reminds us that daily bread would be enough to satisfy—to bring about contentment. Agur's mention of this daily bread has a slightly different connotation than the daily bread Jesus asked for in his teaching prayer of Matthew 6:11. In the original language, Agur's request seems to encompass a bit more, as if he makes a vow to God: "Whatever you have in store for me on any given day, I accept." Could Agur's prayer become ours? Could we pray a similar prayer? "Keep me in the middle of your care, O God. I'll be content with you as watchman over my affairs."

The temptation to overachieve prevails in many arenas of life besides earning wages. In some corporate and social circles, we're expected—perhaps even required—to continually climb upward to prove our worth. Sports, academics, politics, and other areas of life present unusual challenges to Christ-followers—to set reasonable personal goals without turning the goal into a god. When our hearts respond to the knowledge that only "in him we live and move and have our being" (Acts 17:28), we can relax and gain more contentment.

One natural disaster—whether it be earthquake, tornado, flash flood, hurricane, or forest fire—can wipe out a lifetime of achievements in mere minutes. Or men's sins—greed, war, arson, or theft—can cause tangled debacles that cause us to lose our health or loved ones. But if we consistently, sincerely, and passionately make the same worthy plea that the ancient sage Agur made, God can ably keep lies away and help us climb down from worldly pedestals to better roles of godly servants.

- Serve one Master—God.
- Rub shoulders with God to recognize truth.
- Allow your soul to shine.

Undoing Bedazzle

Meditate on this pertinent "don't" from Jesus: "Do not store up for yourselves treasures on earth, where moth and rust destroy, and where thieves break in and steal." Jesus then goes beyond his "don't" to an imperative: "But store up for yourselves treasures in heaven" (Matt. 6:19-20). Almost everyone desires happiness and contentment. The difference comes in where we seek it. To fill their "happy" quota, the dissatisfied mind will seek what the world offers. Christians, however, learn the contentment of righteousness by making deposits in an eternal account.

Though I find great mystery in the phrase "store up for yourselves treasures in heaven," I believe God's vault holds anything I've given over to him. It protects my treasures in a safe place, and I trust Jesus' accounting of cups of cold water given in his name.

Consider the prior week of your life. What did you think about? What motivated your activities each day? What underlying incentives fueled your work? Stop. Pray for honest assessments, and then take a couple of minutes to review your week. And when you're through, read 1 John 2:15-17 from the Amplified Version (AMV) below:

> Do not love or cherish the world or the things that are in the world. If anyone loves the world, love for the Father is not in him. For all that is in the world—the lust of the flesh [craving for sensual gratification] and the lust of the eyes [greedy longings of the mind] and the pride of life [assurance in one's own resources or in the stability of earthly things]—these do not come from the Father but are from the world [itself]. And the world passes away and disappears, and with it the forbidden cravings (the passionate desires, the lust) of it; but he who does the will of God and carries out His purposes in his life abides (remains) forever.

When our granddaughter Jolie lost her first tooth on a Saturday, she found four quarters under her pillow on Sunday morning. She told her dad and mom that she wanted to put them all in "that plate at church." During worship, she held the four quarters in one hand. Soon, she had separated the amount in half, holding two in each hand. When the collection plate finally passed in front of her, she looked into her palms and dropped in one coin. From the Tooth Fairy's purse to God's treasury—I love it! Her giving twenty-five percent, while still generous, reflects our human cravings to rely on what we have in our hands.

Jesus understood the stronghold of flesh on a soul better than any of us comprehend from an earthly perspective. He knows that even at a young age, we become fascinated with ownership. He knows that ownership causes problems if not addressed with his holy help. But even while we dwell in the flesh, he battles alongside us to settle our hearts on the thoughts and will of God. We can win victories over wrong yearnings when we put our confidence in the faithfulness of our Father: "If God is for us, who can be against us?" (Rom. 8:31).

Jesus' words remind us that "where your treasure is, there your heart will be also" (Matt. 6:21). True treasures—our God, our Savior, our blessed Holy Spirit, our salvation—outlive our mortality. Those valuables bring lasting contentment. Nothing, absolutely nothing of this earth compares to those.

Enough Already!

Treasures laid up on earth occupy our time and take up space. Certainly, our possessions assist our living and hospitality, but when we oversupply ourselves, we disturb our contentment. The overseeing of too many goods can cause us to shove aside the command to love the Lord your God with all your heart, with your entire mind, and with all your strength.

In the movie *Sabrina*, the title character gives an impromptu photography lesson to multimillionaire Linus. Holding her camera, he gazes at a landscape through the lens, naming the many possible scenes to photograph. Sabrina removes the camera from his hand saying, "More isn't always best, Linus. Sometimes it's just more."

The term "enoughism" first appeared in John Naish's book *Enough: Breaking Free from the World of More*.[2] John Huxley in *The Sydney Morning Herald* refers to "enoughism" as a grab-all term that identifies the rejection of materialism, "in both the greedy consumption and workaholic acquisition of wealth."[3]

Enoughism says that once people have gained what they need that anything more will complicate their lives. I'm really fond of the term "enoughism." It epitomizes the call I want to answer for my life. I want to draw a definitive line between what I really need, use, and enjoy, and the other stuff that clutters my life. I want to draw a definitive line around the affections of my heart. I long for my affections to settle fully upon God and his purposes. I want to honestly say along with my ancient brother, Asaph, "Whom have I in heaven but you? And being with you, I desire nothing on earth" (Ps. 73:25). I want to live my life in agreement with John's teachings: "The world and its desires pass away, but the man who does the will of God lives forever" (1 John 2:17).

Discontentment usually accompanies the owning of too many possessions. Do you ever step around clutter in your home, office, or business and feel frustrated? Would you let a house guest look into your clothes closet? What lurks in the depths of your refrigerator? Just how many junk drawers do you have?

Do you avoid inviting people into your work office for a conference? Does the top of your desk look like a stacker-sandwich about to topple? If you're not an office worker, what does your workshop or outdoor work area say about you? How well do you function if "chaos" describes your work station?

If you have a garage, do you actually park your vehicles in it—or do you fill it with other items you rarely use? Have the contents of your garage spilled over into your yard? Has indoor furniture homesteaded on your porch? Do you dare to walk barefoot in your yard? Is your automobile tidy? Can you see the floorboard of your car?

Bottom line: How much stuff do you own *anyway*? If you are like me, you answered "Too much!" When I walk into a room of my home where too many things have accummulated, I want to shut down. I stall out. I'm stymied by the mess. How about you? Does your personal world consist of too much stuff or junk areas that would better serve you if they were put on a diet and came out lean?

To let go of our stuff is difficult. Cyndy Salzmann, known as "America's Clutter Coach," reminds in her presentations, "You are not your stuff." She also teaches that when we hang onto things that are no longer useful, they can become our idols.[4] So, I must ask myself, and maybe you could ask yourself, too: What is your most treasured possession? Could you let go of it? What are the less treasured items that clutter your life? Could you let go of them?

The title of Oswald Chamber's book, *My Utmost for Your Highest*, calls me to an ideal. Before I even opened the book and read his encouragement for laying my all on the altar, I understood from the title that he wanted to live out his best life for God's causes. I want the same thing—to put God first and to detach from the perks of the world. But consumer-cultures tout the message that more brings contentment. Elise Boulding says that materialism promotes a lie: "The consumption society has made us feel that happiness lies in having things, and has failed to teach us the happiness of not having things."[5]

Maybe you live with a minimum of possessions, but many of us don't. Let's explore in the next section some practical ways to purge our places and shake out the welcome mat for contentment to come on in. Remember:

- Jesus can cure earth-bedazzlements.
- Store treasures in heaven's safe.
- Adopt "enoughism" as a motto.
- Do your best for God's cause.

Decluttering

If you have decided that your possessions own you instead of you owning your possessions, then you most likely have clutter in your life. Even though you know you have too much, you may still find it difficult to get rid of items.

First, pray for wisdom that God will truly open your eyes so that you may see the things that hinder you. Also, ask for the power to let go. My largest drawback from letting go of things was scheduling time to clean out. When I did finally begin the process of paring down possessions, these other hindrances surfaced—I didn't want to waste resources by throwing things away, and some items had powerful memories attached.

Here's the best advice I've received over the years about scheduling time to clean out. First, you don't need a week, a day, or hours. You only need a few minutes to clean out one drawer or one shelf. When we make excuses of too little time to pare down, we may be avoiding decisions about getting rid of things or letting go.

When you finally begin, have a trash can and a give away container nearby. While waiting for the soup to simmer, use those moments to clean out one small area of your kitchen. Spend part of your coffee break at work cleaning out one desk drawer.

Some people like to have garage or rummage sales, and I've had my share of those, but the less complicated way to be rid of things is to give them away. You could also have a freebie garage sale. No pricing, no having to make change, just give things away.

When I clean out, I don't make several stacks to disperse elsewhere (give to friends, see if this or that person could use an item). Even that gets too complicated. I just ask the Lord's forgiveness for overbuying and I put it into my give-away bag.

Not wanting to waste, I've found local donation centers happy to accept my misguided purchases or good condition items no longer of use to my family. Some of my favorite places to donate extras include an assistance league, where I see bargain hunters shopping. Another thrift store where I donate not only hires recovering addicts, they also provide on-site housing and discipling for their employees.

The Freecycle Network, a worthy group with worldwide free membership, helps keep landfills free of useable items by giving things away among members. My friend received a beautiful dollhouse for her girls' Christmas when someone's daughter outgrew it. Freecycle stemmed from a grass-roots movement and remains a not-for-profit organization. When I received my membership welcome letter, it encouraged, "Free your inner packrat." Find The Freecycle Network at www.freecycle.org.[6]

Order in the home will mean different things to different people, but each person or family needs to have enough order so that the family can function easily. That means without frantic searches for lost keys and misplaced items. That means that tennis shoes and socks, books, bags, and lunches reside in specific places. That means your family can function without messy areas and flaring tempers.

Mindy Starns Clark gives great guidelines for homes in her book, *The House That Cleans Itself*. She says that everything we own—from the tiniest button to the largest piece of furniture—requires an investment of our time.

As we declutter we make room for learning contentment instead of giving into frazzled feelings. Mrs. Clark suggests asking the following questions for each article we own:

- "Is this item worth my time?"
- "Does what I get from this item provide a fair trade-off considering I have to clean it and store it?"
- "Do I want to spend a single second in the future fooling with it, or do I want to get rid of it now so it will no longer cost me a thing?"[7]

Great questions, Mindy. If we can answer them correctly and act on our answers, we can free up our lives from the unnecessary.

As for things we cling to for sentimental reasons, each person will need to decide what to keep and if it's time to give any of those things away. I've already passed along some things to my son and daughter and to friends. I'm holding onto other things I still enjoy having around. However, I understand that while they bring joy to me, my children may not have the same association with the object. My oversized cornbread pan with folded corners holds a tiny portion of my heart because my grandmother used it for her large family, and an old blacksmith they knew had made it. Knowing I love to cook, she personally handed it to me one of the last times I saw her.

Realizing that some of our sentimental treasures may not hold any charm for our descendents, we can unclutter our spaces and pass them along to someone who will get some use of them or enjoy them.

- Schedule time to clear out your space.
- Learn to let go.
- Declutter to allow your household to function effectively.

An Underlying Purpose of Learning Contentment

I'm acquainted with Christians who have obviously learned content-ment. They show me the nature of Christ in their actions and the settled calm of their souls. Their quiet confidence that God always takes care of them draws me nearer to living out a similar faith. I know many such people, and I recognize the draw that calm Christians have upon fraz-zled people.

I recall a couple of stories about my parents and their obvious detach-ment from things. While they built their home from their savings plus a small bank loan, they lived in a travel trailer on their two lots. Due to a lack of space, they moved their household furnishings to a storage facility. Dad worked through the day at his regular job and then built their house in the evenings and on weekends (when they weren't conducting home Bible studies or helping someone else).

While I talked to Mom one day before she became ill, she casually mentioned a struggling family who had lost everything. Concerned for the family, I asked how they were going to make it. She said, "Daddy and I let them have our refrigerator and anything else they needed from our storage unit." I knew my parents were on a tight budget and didn't have much spare money for new things.

I shook my head in disbelief, and said, "Mom, your house will be ready to move into soon. What will you do?"

She simply said, "The Lord will provide." And we never talked about it again. And when they moved into their new home—quite less than finished—they bought second-hand furniture as funds allowed, and they continued their hospitality to strangers and saints alike.

On another occasion, they found out about a family member who needed transportation. Dad said this about their second vehicle, "I wish we were financially able to let them have it."

Mom replied in two words, "We are." And, with Mom's simple affirmation of her contentment with their "riches," Dad phoned to let my aunt know they now had a vehicle. In many ways, my parents didn't set their affections on things below, so the letting go was much easier. Over the years, many witnessed my parents' devotion and obedience to the Lord. With Mom's illness, my contented Dad still conducts home Bible studies, guiding many to Christ.

As long as we live, we can either tangle with possessions or make them serve us to bring glory to God.

- "You are not your stuff."
- Get rid of clutter.
- Set your affections on things above.

Welcome the Lord's peace that passes understanding. Your peace, shining out for all to see, in turn welcomes a troubled world to discover the source of your joy. When overachievers and over-possessors witness your learned contentment—in various stages for each of us—take the opportunity to share the hope you have in Christ.

God can keep you strong in your resolve to live life to the fullest and yet keep possessions at a manageable level.

Embracing Contentment
Jennifer Slattery's Story

My husband and I led a Bible study on how to manage finances from a biblical perspective, and I thought I had this whole contentment thing down. Sure, I
struggled occasionally—like when I'd drive by one of those multi-million dollar
houses overlooking the lake or when I'd see a friend wearing shoes I couldn't
afford. But for the most part, I was pretty happy, and grateful for all that God
had blessed us with.

We weren't rich, but we had all we needed, and more important, we had
each other. What more could we ask for? And oh, how I loved to recite, "I know
what it is to be in need, and I know what it is to have plenty. I have learned the
secret of being content in any and every situation" (Phil. 4:12). Paul's words were
especially handy when my husband longed for the latest golf club or high tech
electronic gadget. I truly thought I'd learned to be content in whatever situation—with or without that trendy new blouse I saw down at the mall.

But things happen and incomes change. Six months later when the stakes
rose to "cutting our losses and running to higher ground," my grateful contentment soon gave way to grasping, reaching, whining, and complaining.

Bitterness nearly consumed me. It just wasn't fair! We didn't deserve this. God
had let us down. It would take me two more months and a jog through inner city
Corpus Christi for God to change my heart so I could learn true contentment.

After working for the railroad for twenty-four years, my husband suddenly
found himself unemployed. Despite all of the résumés sent out, he couldn't find
anything permanent. After blasting through our savings, we came to the realization that we would need to sell our house—the house that God had blessed
us with less than a year before.

What he had given to us, what we had thanked and praised him for, was
suddenly being taken away. Desperate to earn money in any way possible, my
husband took a temporary, contract job six hours away. He left on Sunday

nights, stayed in a hotel paid for by his new employer, and then headed home on Fridays, only to do it all over again come Sunday.

My daughter and I remained in our home, and I did everything I could to sell our house. Within a few short weeks, it sold for considerably less than we paid. A few days later, I stood in front of a ten by fifteen foot storage unit and watched sweaty men place most of our belongings inside. Then my daughter and I drove to our five-hundred-square-foot, one-bedroom, temporary apartment.

To say I was bitter is an understatement. To be honest, my bitterness surprised me. I thought I had a grasp on contentment, but I struggled over losing our house in the nice little neighborhood. And even worse, I didn't want anyone to see where or how we lived in our cramped quarters. I felt embarrassed about our new living conditions—my daughter sleeping on the living room couch and our basic needs scattered across dingy carpets.

My sister lived a few hours away, and since my daughter and I had an entire summer to kill, we drove south for a visit—and a break from reality. While there, I went for a jog. In an unfamiliar city this probably wasn't the best idea, but I needed some "me" time. I laced on a pair of shoes and headed for the road. I ran and ran and ran. Crying out to God, I threw my own pity party.

Caught up in my downward spiral, I got lost in a run-down part of town. Instead of nice trimmed hedges and lawns, houses were surrounded by cracked dirt and overgrown weeds. Chain link fences lay on the ground and many house windows were boarded.

But the landscape of faces caught my attention: Children wore huge smiles as they sat on front steps or played in dirt-packed yards. I watched a father and his two children play in water sprayed from a simple garden hose. I suddenly realized just how dark my heart had become.

I had allowed myself to become miserable because we had had to sell our house. But the families I viewed, who lived in perhaps one of the poorest areas of Texas, laughed as if they hadn't a care in the world. That's when a realization hit me. I saw an accurate portrait of contentment—and even more importantly, what experiencing contentment could do for me and my family.

I had a choice to make. I could either continue to wallow in self-pity, feeding my bitterness one negative thought at a time, or I could turn my eyes heavenward and focus on the gifts God had given me, allowing his joy and peace to wash over me like a cleansing river.

Three years have passed since that eye-opening day. God in his mercy has restored much of what we lost. A new perspective has gripped me, and I enjoy the wonderful gifts God has given—but my enjoyment is different, more tempered. God allowed us to remain a family even though we had many possessions stripped away. I've learned how unnecessary temporary trappings really are. I know how quickly life can change, and I have learned to hold possessions more loosely.

The best thing of all? This new casual grip allows me to truly enjoy the Giver more than the gifts.

Memorize and pray these scriptures to assist in freedom from overachievement and over-possession.

Praise: "He brought me out into a spacious place; he rescued me because he delighted in me" (2 Sam. 22:20).

Petition: "And this is my prayer: that [my] love may abound more and more in knowledge and depth of insight, so that [I] may be able to discern what is best and may be pure and blameless until the day of Christ" (Phil. 1:9).

As you consider the questions, remember:

- The world allures.
- Overachievement harms the soul.
- Possessions can vanish in a moment.
- "Enoughism" defines a worthy goal.
- Freedom comes with owning less.

1. Have you seen lives ruined because someone gave in to overachieving? Keeping in mind the motivation of Agur's prayer (Prov. 30:7-9), do you think middle-of-the road living is an okay place to reside?

2. People around us may see only the outward sparkle of the put-together person we choose to present to them. What does Jesus' statement mean to you: "[L]et your light shine before men, that they may see your good deeds and praise your Father in heaven" (Matt. 5:16)?

3. Which scripture reference in this chapter tugged at your heart? Allow the Bible words further voice by writing them on an index card, and then place those words in a prominent place so God can continue to coach you through them.

4. How has Luke 12:15 proved truthful to your life, "[A] man's life does not consist in the abundance of his possessions"?

5. "As goods increase, so do those who consume them. And what benefit are they to the owner except to feast his eyes on them?" (Eccles. 5:11). Recall an impulse buy that quickly lost its luster? How can you avoid impulse buys in the future?

6. "The commands of the LORD are radiant, giving light to the eyes" (Ps. 19:8). Our radiance—that shines out to others—comes from the Lord. How has your soul shined to others this week?

7. "Death and Destruction are never satisfied, and neither are the eyes of man" (Prov. 27:20). Do you have your heart set upon getting something in this world—furnishings, finer clothes, a newer car, or house? Pray and discover if those are real needs that will assist you in making God look good to others (bringing glory to God) or making self look good?

8. Through Amos, the Lord told the house of Israel, to "Seek me and live; do not seek Bethel [counterfeits]" (5:5). Word a simple prayer asking God to help you discern between counterfeits and everlasting matters.

LIVING FROM SCAN
TO SCAN
When the Unthinkable Happens

When times are good, be happy; but when times are bad, consider:
God has made the one as well as the other.

Ecclesiastes 7:14

everly Grayson has experienced more suffering than some and less
than others. We've met in person only twice, but through internet connections, we became fast friends.

You know how it happens. First, you meet someone. Then, as you get
to know one another, each of your stories unfolds. I met Beverly when I presented the topic "Praying in the Name of Jesus" at Pepperdine University
annual lectures. After the class, as we talked about several similarities in
our lives, we "connected." When she returned to Tennessee, she requested that her home congregation women's ministry invite me to speak at
their spring women's renewal. Later, my daughter and I flew from Texas
to Nashville. During that trip, our acquaintance deepened to a friendship.

After the event in Tennessee, we began to email back and forth.
Through that regular correspondence, we learned even more about each
others' families, backgrounds, and how Jesus shaped our faith. In this
chapter, you'll read about Beverly's current journey. We'll also consider

the types of suffering and loss we might experience in life, and how God especially infuses mercy into even the dark moments, hours, or years. No one escapes suffering, but we'll discover how God blends peace into those intimidating circumstances.

Beverly's Current Story

Although a grandmother and a sister in Beverly's family died of cancer, Beverly seemed in perfect health when a slight problem landed her in the doctor's office in 2004. Much to her surprise, when tests results came back, she found out that she had developed a malignancy, a rare mixed Mullerian tumor (MMT).

In 2010, she began her sixth round of medical treatments and chemo. That's when Beverly created her blog, "John's Wife." There, she chronicles her joy, favorite scriptures, and illness, so other cancer patients can have a place of community. She admits her journey isn't always one of happiness, "but during these days I have gained strength from God, the Bible, Christian friends, and family. I have good days and bad days—it's scary, but I would like to share this journey . . . ."

After her initial treatments and surgeries, she felt hopeful about her health, but even then she kept hearing a very tiny voice asking, "Is it back?" But Beverly says she "always hoped for the best, to find a cure, and achieve a life of normalcy."

In one blog entry, Beverly shares about a bracelet she wears bearing this inscription: "With God all Things are Possible." She wears it "every day, to show the world I believe this to be true."[1] Beverly said that the message on the bracelet rejuvenates her with the same God-assurance sent to Mary by way of the angel Gabriel: "With God, nothing shall be impossible" (Luke 1:37 KJV).

Even though Beverly has gone through many treatments, the cancer continues to threaten her life. When she began her fourth round of treatment, Beverly and her husband John downsized and built an apartment onto their daughter's home. I admire Beverly's devotion to family, God, and his Holy Bible. Later in this chapter, you'll read her personal essay about her early marriage—and especially how her study of God's word contributed to the contentment God has given her.

"In This World You Will Have Trouble."

On the night before his arrest, Jesus taught his disciples, issuing hope and a warning. Best of all, he offered himself as a place of refuge: "I have told you these things, so that in me you may have peace. In this world you will have trouble. But take heart! I have overcome the world" (John 16:33). I'm fond of every teaching in those words except the stated truth that "in this world you will have trouble." I don't like trouble!

But, like it or not, a "world of trouble" is our current physical address. Until the Lord's return, we will experience fallout from the Garden of Eden. Acknowledging that life will not be perfect remains the first step to surviving rounds of suffering and losses.

Jesus encouraged his disciples to "take heart!" When we *take* courage from Jesus, we not only endure suffering, but we can also shine through it for him. God compares one who has trust and confidence in him as a well-watered tree—it "does not fear when heat comes; its leaves are always green. It has no worries in a year of drought and never fails to bear fruit" (Jer. 17:7-8).

Let's compare the types of agonies we might endure and the biblical characters who suffered similarly because their examples can aid us to look for and find God's help in comparable circumstances.

One—Sin, Death, and Briar Suffering

Loss, pain, anguish, torment, affliction—call it what you want, but it hurts. For this chapter, I name eight types of suffering that could happen to Christians. Of course, within each division, many sub-categories—as diverse as the population of the earth—could exist.

The first category, "Sin, Death, and Briar Suffering," refers to the pain of sin, death, and toil that stems from sin's initial entry into the world. Near the beginning of time, sin entered unlocking a Pandora's Box of hurt and suffering. When sin and the resulting sentence of death became part of our existence, so did other harsh—even dangerous and devastating—realities: Adam no longer picked fruit from trees that God planted; he'd toil and sweat to harvest another fig or grape crop.

Because of sin, Eve delivered her babies in excruciating pain. The severe birth process ensured long careers for midwives, obstetricians, and anesthesiologists. And, even the earth changed nature at God's command. Instead of a tranquil garden, a briar patch took over. I can identify with this reality. Every time I try to eradicate the wild rose bushes on our farm, I am reminded of our fallen nature. We suffer back-aching work in yards and acreages in our attempts to stall briar growth for even one growing season.

Even though a gavel of death fell upon the world—"For the wages of sin is death"—God had pre-constructed an escape, a "gift of God . . . eternal life in Christ Jesus our Lord" (Rom. 6:23). Sin has an innate trickle down effect that creates many sufferings. Let's consider some others.

Two—Surprise Suffering

Surprise suffering occurs when we are injured or suffer loss through a circumstance we could not foresee or avoid. Sometimes, bad things happen, and it's no one's fault. It's just an accident. Surprise suffering could include any of the following:

- A banana peel causes a fall.
- An employer goes out of business, leaving employees out of work.
- A limb falls from a tree and injures someone standing underneath.

Why did a plane with motor problems and an oil splashed windshield land on the stretch of coastline exactly where a young father exercised his morning run? He left a wife, his children, and his mother in a wake of grief. Solomon witnessed the same kind of arbitrary suffering: "The race is not to the swift or the battle to the strong, nor does food come to the wise or wealth to the brilliant or favor to the learned; but time and chance happen to them all" (Eccles. 9:11).

Surprise suffering happens in the blink of an eye. And the victim's world changes. The suffering might be temporary, such as an illness and the return of good health, or it could be something that will never vary and will affect the dynamics of life forever.

Three—Suffering at the Hands of Others

This third area of pain occurs when someone sins and we experience the effects of that sin. Friends of ours lost a son and young grandson because someone drove drunk and hit their family car one sunny afternoon. When a dad or mom gives in to verbal abuse of children, they destroy fragile egos and precious opportunities. Or what about those times when a thief has taken a precious belonging? Or when someone defrauds health providers, we all pay.

Read 2 Samuel 21 to get another picture of suffering at the hands of someone else. The biblical character Rizpah suffered because of King Saul's sins. Rizpah was one of Saul's many concubines—essentially a willing or unwilling mistress. She bore him two sons, Armoni and Mephibosheth. Because King Saul broke an old covenant, the offended Gibeonites demanded retribution after his death. Soon, Rizpah's two sons and the five sons of Saul's daughter Merab were killed, their bodies exposed to the elements. But Rizpah kept watch over her sons' bodies from harvest to the rainy season, determined that neither fowl nor beast molest them. Her story implies that King David came to her rescue and buried her sons.

Rizpah suffered tremendous pain due to others' sins.

Four—Suffering Because of My Sins

We also reap consequences from the sins we sow. Consider these words of renowned preacher Marshall Keeble: "Sin will take you further than you'll ever want to go, keep you longer, and cost you more than you ever want to pay." When we overeat, we reap extra poundage. When we lie to our mate, their trust in us falters. When we ignore solitude, we reap a frazzled life.

In my devotional book, *The Stained Glass Pickup*, I included a meditation entitled "One More Night with Frogs." When given the opportunity to set the time for the removal of the plague of frogs, Pharaoh said, "Tomorrow." To me, those invasive frogs symbolized sins. Here's an excerpt:

> Like frogs, sins creep in and cling. Some offenders try to hide their sins from spouse, coworkers, children, community, or church. Hidden indiscretions range from cheating on income taxes to cheating in marriage, from stealing pencils to embezzling, from slothful parenting to abuse, from neglect of others to indulgence of self. . . .
>
> Secret sin rarely stays secret; it has a way of hopping to headline news. Any sin produces rotten fruit, and—over time—contaminates the life of the perpetrator. Sins seem to have their own pride, and sooner or later they boast or leave telltale signs in their host.[2]

If I commit murder, I pay the penalty required by law. If I display pride, I reap disgrace (Prov. 11:2). If I covet my neighbor's car or house or husband, I darken my soul. Every sin has corresponding consequences. It may be an internal darkening or an outward display that affects my family and community. Whether sins hide in secret or broadcast blatant acts of disobedience, they never fool God.

"If the righteous receive their due on earth, how much more the ungodly and the sinner!" (Prov. 11:31).

Five—Choosing to Suffer

The fifth suffering encompasses those times when we choose a noble path, even knowing that we will reap some sort of hardship. Think of a caring church friend who volunteers to sit up with an ill person at night. She chooses to lose sleep and possibly get behind on her chores. Similarly, even a blood or platelet donor spends an hour or more to "Give the gift of life." Missionaries help the cause of Christ in foreign lands—many times thousands of miles away from their families.

Life will present opportunities to ease another's burden—often at some cost to us. Sometimes benevolence halts our lives for a few days. Or it might take years of involvement to see someone to a safer place in their health or spiritual life. At other times this kind of suffering involves what Jesus calls "greater love." We might even lay down our lives so that others may survive. Battlefields resound with such stories.

Jesus set the supreme example when he chose to suffer. He chose to come to earth, he chose to lay down his life day-by-day for others, and he chose to comply with the worst possible death imaginable. "'*Abba*, Father,' Jesus prayed, 'everything is possible for you. Take this cup from me. Yet not what I will, but what you will'" (Mark 14:36).

"Greater love has no one than this, that one lay down his life for his friends" (John 15:13).

Six— Suffering the Discipline of God

Solomon instructed his son: "[D]o not despise the Lord's discipline and do not resent his rebuke, because the LORD disciplines those he loves, as a father the son he delights in" (Prov. 3:11-12). The author of Hebrews expanded on Solomon's teaching by saying that no discipline is pleasant, but rather it is painful, even though God disciplines us for our good. We're advised that the discipline of the Lord remains vital to our training. What should we do when God disciplines us? Repent. Submit. What should we expect to gain? Additional training from God. What is produced? A harvest of righteousness and peace (Heb. 12:5-12).

Seven—Out-of-Relationship-with-Jesus Suffering

The seventh and eighth categories of sufferings are exclusive to Christians. Christians live with deep pain when a person dear to them refuses to allow Jesus into their heart. Even though God tugs at the heart of the lost, and arranges attention-getters, the loved one may remain aloof, ignoring his love.

Even in such circumstances, we know that God desires to have them in relationship, immeasurably more than we do. God assures us of his love for the lost through the giving of his son as a ransom for all. Father and Son don't want any to perish apart from them (John 3:16-17). God treks after one wandering lamb (Matt. 18:12-14). I personally abide in the hope that God will keep someone alive as long as the potential exists for turning to him. I take comfort in the instruction of the wise woman of Tekoa—that God "devises ways so that a banished person may not remain estranged from him" (2 Sam. 14:14). I believe her statement proves true through other biblical stories such as Adam and Eve, Saul of Tarsus, the Philippian jailer, the centurion Cornelius, the Ethiopian eunuch—to name just a few.

Eight—Suffering for Christ's Sake

The truth of this suffering can be tracked throughout scripture. Paul often suffered for the cause of Christ, which probably came as no surprise to him. As Paul made his way to Damascus to persecute Christians, Jesus appeared and commissioned him: "I have appeared to you to appoint you as a servant and as a witness" (Acts 26:16). Paul later wrote to Timothy: "In fact, everyone who wants to live a godly life in Christ Jesus will be persecuted" (2 Tim. 3:12).

When we walk in the light—the Way—we become beacons of spiritual truths. When a light comes in contact with darkness, the light will of its own accord invade and disturb darkness.

From my experience, darkness fights back, often resulting in persecution or slander. Following Jesus' law-of-love, we allow our lights to shine, not in pride, but a genuine I-care-about-you way. Wickedness has its own love-party going on and lashes back at God. But we've witnessed people encountering God's goodness and being led toward repentance (Rom. 2:4).

God the Father and Jesus the Son engaged in this battle long before we joined their ranks. Jesus encourages us to stand fast because "[b]lessed are those who are persecuted because of righteousness, for theirs is the kingdom of heaven" (Matt. 5:10). Jesus further said that because of our connection to him, we'll receive insults and people will make up all kinds of false things about us. "Rejoice and be glad" because a great reward awaits us.

Imagine this scene: a battle between good and evil takes place, with the captains picking team members. Suddenly, Jesus points at you, calls you by name and picks you to be on the winning team. With Jesus as captain, we can accept the times of suffering for his team. We can rejoice and place our hope in victory. John, exiled on the isle of Patmos, did just that. Paul chained to a Roman guard did. Jesus' mother did. She watched her son and her Lord endure excruciating pain—as the painful prophecy of Simeon came true, "a sword will pierce your own soul too" (Luke 2:35). But God soon gifted her and all those persecuted early believers with his Holy Spirit. And the Holy Spirit helped them remember the teachings of Jesus and their implications.

Like those early believers and followers, we accept the peace and joy that Jesus pours into our lives in the middle of debilitating persecutions. After being flogged, "The apostles left the Sanhedrin, rejoicing because they had been counted worthy of suffering disgrace for the Name" (Acts 5:41).

Coping with Suffering

Have you heard someone ask, "How do people who don't know God get through tragedies?" I've often wondered the same. One day I made a similar remark to Jill Pryor, a new convert. She related to me a before and after picture. She said that before she became a follower of Christ that she just plodded through, trying to outlast and get to the other side of everyday mishaps and larger disasters.

Jill said, "I just didn't know anything better was out there." Her answer brought both sadness and joy—sadness for those without Jesus, and gratitude that now Jill is friends with Jesus, who has helped her through personal losses. Since she became a Christian, the trials haven't stopped, but she has shown an indomitable trust in Jesus.

However, even though we've turned our lives over to Jesus, sometimes we try to take back the reins. David Bivin, of Jerusalem, Israel, diagnoses Christians working from their own strength with the "Samson syndrome."[3] It seems that's what Judge Samson did. For his early life, he obeyed God and kept his oaths, but when he tangled with foreign women—not of his faith—his choices brought about all sorts of dilemmas. He ended up stripped of his God-given muscular strength, blind, and shackled with bronze cuffs to a grinding wheel. God mercifully answered Samson's final prayer for help, and many cruelties to his countrymen and himself were avenged (Judg. 13-16).

Even though we know that suffering is inevitable, we should not walk around fearing the worst. That's not God's intended path for us. Jesus warned us of trouble and so did Solomon: "When times are good be happy; but when times are bad consider: God has made the one as well as the other" (Eccles. 7:14).

Drs. Jerry and Lynn Jones present "Marriage Matters" conferences across our nation. My home congregation hosted their seminar, and in one session Lynn spoke to an audience for women only. She reminded us that God molds us to be like Jesus—through blessings and adversities. She summed up with this statement, "My God is not a pampering god, but a perfecting God."

In our tempests, God remains as constant as he did in Job's; remember that God spoke to him "out of the storm" (Job 38:1; 40:6). Hearing the voice of God during our trials and deaths of people we love, we do not grieve as others who have no hope. However, we still grieve over losses (1 Thess. 4:13). We're human, and we can expect suffering to hurt. But we can also expect supernatural help in coping.

So how do we make it through when minor mishaps occur or calamity strikes? Many Bible heroes and heroines set the stage—they sought God. God said to those in Isaiah's day, "Give ear and come to me; hear me, that your soul may live" (Isa. 55:3).

In sufferings, don't abandon your quest for God. Keep pursuing him, and he will be found. God—the force that calms winds and waters—can reach down and hold us upright; he can hold our heads above the water. Tim Hansel says, "We must take our Theology and make it our Biography."[4]

My friend Beverly Grayson has done just that. Even in the middle of suffering, even when the unthinkable happens in her life, she relies on the word of God and his blessed Holy Spirit to keep shaping her into the image of Christ. Even in her latest battle with cancer, her contentment and trust shine through in what she once said to me: "I'm just living from scan to scan, from grace to grace."

Embracing Contentment
Beverly Grayson's Story

I had it all in my near perfect childhood—a big collie, horses, and plenty of woods and fields to roam. My loving parents took me to church, and at the tender age of nine, I gave my life to Christ. That's when I developed my lifelong habit of daily Bible reading. Little did I know how that habit would carry me through many trials.

I married soon after I graduated high school, at age seventeen. Our first baby, Jimmy, came along nine months later. When I was twenty-one, our second son Johny arrived. Johny weighed only 5 lbs. 3 oz., and his small size caused multiple problems: he caught viral pneumonia at six weeks and strep throat at three months; he also developed nephritis; and had a chronic kidney disorder for the next two years. He could not eat from a spoon because of a sensitive gag reflex, and he took daily growth hormone and penicillin for two years. We realized he was delayed in both mental and developmental skills.

The next eight years brought more changes: I suffered a miscarriage; my husband John lost his job (and got another one); my sons had their tonsils removed, and we had a baby girl, Cathy. During those years, we went to numerous doctors trying to find a diagnosis for Johny's condition.

Caring for three children kept me busy, and we had money problems, due in part to Johny's three surgeries. Eventually, we lost our home and moved into John's parents' home. They graciously let us live there, and they found another place to live.

Johny's lack of good health pressed me with guilt. "Why, God—did I not get the right nutrition during my pregnancy? Did Johny catch that early viral pneumonia at the church nursery?"

Along with other difficulties, our home life deteriorated. The children fought constantly. Even going to church proved disastrous. I spent many years in the cry room, because Johny and little Cathy could not sit through the worship service without disrupting others. Although he was now nine, Johny still behaved like a two-year-old. Family outings, except for camping, were almost impossible. My guilt remained. During those years, my Bible reading was a "constant" that held me together.

We finally built a home next door to my in-laws. The children had plenty of room to run on their land, along with the bonus of grandparents living so close.

Finally, at age ten, Johny was diagnosed as brain damaged. A psychologist advised us to take care of the rest of our family too. He saw the suffering in

John, me, Jimmy, and Cathy. More guilt jumped on my back. More questions: "Why, God? What did I do wrong?"

After much soul searching, we decided to find an alternate living situation for Johny. We looked for a boarding school for two years and finally found Orange Grove School in Chattanooga, Tennessee. A private school with high expenses, I needed to find a way to help pay for twelve-year-old Johny's tuition, room, and board. By that time, Jimmy was fourteen and Cathy was nine.

When Johny moved away to boarding school, a major change in our family dynamics took place. At the time, I thought this to be the most traumatic thing that would ever happen in our lives. My mother-heart felt as if I had cast my Johny out of our home!

Johny needed long-term training in school which meant I needed a job. I wanted to teach, so for six years I worked days as a school secretary and went to college at night. My dear husband John came home to finish the dinner I'd started, help with homework, and clean the house. He was my rock during this time.

Johny was very unhappy for several years, and it tore at my heart to leave him at school. Once a month, we picked him up on Friday afternoons and took him back on Sunday night. Every time, we left him crying, and I cried as we drove the four hours back home. On each trip, the same agonizing question resurfaced, "Why, God?"

Even with our tight schedules, our home life improved. Throughout this time—children growing up, leaving home, going away to college—I wondered why God chose us to be Johny's parents. Why did we have such money problems when all our friends seemed to have perfect children, fine homes, boats, new cars, and all the things I believed made a happy life? During those years and my questioning, I still read my Bible each day.

Looking back, I know God walked with us all the way, and we saw many resulting blessings. All my college classes were offered in time slots that worked for our family. When I graduated, a job awaited me. Our oldest son was appointed to West Point Military Academy, partly as a result of a friend I met in college. And, miracle of miracles, as Johny grew older he went to "work" in a sheltered workshop. He took pride in his $6.00 weekly paycheck. He continued to live under the supervision of the school, but he learned to ride the Greyhound Bus to come home.

In his early twenties, Johny wanted to be baptized. Although we knew that Jesus saw our precious son as saved, we welcomed this act of faith for Johny's satisfaction.

Johny never read or wrote anything except his name. He never had any concept of money or math. But he had such integrity. He was honest; he never lied; he possessed a strong character. He was a fun-loving and very social young man. He showed us unconditional love and patience. As I saw God's grace-full plan unfold, I finally quit asking "Why God?" I knew we had made the right decision—Johny deserved the independence he worked to earn.

And then the unthinkable happened. Orange Grove School phoned to tell us that Johny had died suddenly while exercising and running on the track. At age twenty-nine our precious son was gone. I'd never known such intense grief. And the questions returned: "God, why did Johny die just as we 'got it all together'?"

A verse from Philippians became my anchor through this extremely rough time. "Do not be anxious about anything, but in everything, by prayer and petition, with thanksgiving, present your requests to God. And the peace of God, which transcends all understanding, will guard your hearts and your minds in Christ Jesus" (4:6). God had always been there for me, always a constant, always present in my Bible reading and studying.

My Bible study didn't bring me all the answers, my questioning God didn't either, but I saw the results of his care. Because of Johny's presence in our lives, our family developed deep compassion—borne from God and from taking care of Johny. Because of Johny, I went to college, taught school, and influenced other children.

Even now, God helps me grow in grace and contentment. God knows my future. And I fully trust—even in this sixth battle with cancer—that "my God will meet all [my] needs according to his glorious riches in Christ Jesus" (Phil. 4:19).

Memorize and pray these verses when faced with an "unthinkable."

Praise: "To him who is able to keep you from falling and to present you before his glorious presence without fault and with great joy" (Jude 24).
Petition: "Turn to me and be gracious to me, for I am lonely and afflicted. The troubles of my heart have multiplied; free me from my anguish" (Ps. 26:16-17).

As you consider the questions, remember:

- In this world you will have trouble.
- Jesus has overcome the world.
- Suffering reveals itself in many ways.
- God works with us through suffering.

1. God compared the faithful to a green tree planted by water: "It has no worries in a year of drought and never fails to bear fruit" (Jer. 17:7-8). During suffering, have you seen this prediction of fruit bearing work out in your life?

2. "The LORD is close to the brokenhearted and saves those who are crushed in spirit. A righteous man may have many troubles, but the LORD delivers him from them all" (Ps. 34:18-19). Some describe their most awful circumstances as a "thin place" where they sensed God's nearness. Give details of a time when God came near to your broken heart?

3. Choose at least one of the eight categories of suffering mentioned in this chapter, and write how God saw you through it. Did you learn a measure of contentment during that time?

4. Paul let the Thessalonians know his prayer for them in his second letter: "May the Lord direct your hearts into God's love and Christ's perseverance" (3:5). Memorize this phrase. This week, pray this

over someone you know is suffering, who needs the Lord's peace and contentment.

5. Read Judges 16, about Samson and Delilah. Match Samson's sufferings to the categories you just read about in this chapter.

6. Have you ever taken back the reins of your life from Jesus and suffered the "Samson syndrome"? How did that work out? Did you turn your life back over to Jesus?

7. Read Job 42, especially meditating upon the epilogue. Job suffered tremendous loss, but in later years all was restored plus more. Calculate how many years the restoration took.

8. Word a simple prayer asking that Jesus' words be kneaded into your mind, heart, and soul this week: "In this world you will have trouble. But take heart! I have overcome the world" (John 16:33).

Chapter Eight

JACOB, GOD HAS A SURPRISE FOR YOU

Confidence in God as Author

[M]ay God Almighty grant you mercy. . . .

Genesis 43:14

One evening, a group of our friends discussed seeing the "Passion Play" in Eureka Springs, Arkansas. Some told of inspirational scenes; others bemoaned the length of time they sat on uncomfortable stadium-type benches with no backs. One person turned to my husband and asked, "Dave, do you think you and Cathy will ever go?"

Dave replied, "Probably not. It always ends the same."

Like Dave, I prefer stories that end on a happy note, the way I want them to. Of course, Jesus' story reigns over all others in terms of ultimately having a good surprise ending. We're so familiar with the resurrection story that we sometimes forget the surprise those early believers experienced when they discovered that Jesus had risen from the dead.

Even though benevolent God authors our lives, we may not see the results we expect. But without hesitation, I can say that, whenever I made a request of God, his surprise solutions remain far superior to my suggested or expected outcomes.

What about you? Do you still have requests awaiting answers? Have you experienced surprise answers to some of your prayers? In this chapter, we'll see the power of trusting in God's navigation. Right now, can you answer yes to these questions: Can I be content with God as author and finisher of my life and faith (Heb. 12:2)? Can my ego be satisfied living out the Christian cliché "Let go and let God"?

Perhaps you and I can better answer those questions after we reflect on Jacob's life-junket. We'll see how God authored and finished his faith, how God sketched in surprises, and how God drew Jacob to himself, the ultimate abiding place of contentment.

Jacob, the Deceiver

I'm pleased that within the Bible God allows us a full—accurate and detailed—picture of some people's lives. Genesis 25-49 gives us information about Jacob's life from birth to death. His back story shows his ancestors relying on God: outside the Garden of Eden (Garden of Delight), after an earth-drowning flood, through hurts and betrayals, and during riffs between kin. Those accounts also reveal joyous moments, such as the births of children and moments of refreshing that came from the Lord. By carefully examining aspects of the beginning, middle, and end of Jacob's story, we can specifically see how God drew him into relationship. Let's start with his parents.

Rebecca and Isaac became husband and wife, but she remained barren for twenty years afterwards. When finally pregnant, she had conceived twin boys, and "[t]he babies jostled each other within her" (25:22). Puzzled by this, Rebecca inquired of the Lord (this could mean she sought counsel from her father-in-law, Abraham, a prophet of God). A prophecy resulted which said that Rebecca's sons would be patriarchs of two nations with the older (Esau) serving the younger (Jacob).

The twins seemed to throw punches at each other while still in the womb, and it would not be much different in life, where their rivalry continued well into their adulthood. During their births, Esau arrived first, but the midwife noticed that the second baby, Jacob, grasped his brother's heel.

The name Jacob literally means "grasps the heel." Figuratively, it means "deceiver." Never was this more evident than when Jacob became of marriageable age and outfoxed his elderly, blind father Isaac to gain his brother's firstborn blessing. When his older brother found out, Esau's fury paved a path for murderous revenge.

In haste, Jacob's parents sent him away to seek a wife among her relatives in Paddan Aram, and Jacob obeyed them out of fear for his life. As he traveled into unknown territory, into an unknown future, I wonder if his previous behavior bothered him. Did he regret lying to his father, scheming to get the best blessing? Was he afraid of the venture he'd been sent upon?

When night descended, he stopped to rest, and chose a stone to pillow his head. Despite Jacob's conniving ways, merciful God delivered a message in a dream—in this case a dream that was both sweet and terrifying at the same time.

Jacob saw a ladder that led from earth to heaven on which angels ascended and descended. From his perch at the top, God said that Jacob's family would be like the dust of the earth, and that all peoples of the earth would be blessed through him. God promised to remain with Jacob and bring him back to the very land he slept upon.

When Jacob awakened, he thought, "Surely the LORD is in this place, and I was not aware of it" (28:16). Then the text says he was afraid, but he finally gained his voice. I imagine if you see God in a dream, you have to tell someone about the experience, even if you simply say it aloud to yourself: "How awesome is this place! This is none other than the house of God; this is the gate of heaven" (28:17).

Jacob stood the stone-pillow upright and anointed it, marking the personal historic site. Afterward, he made a vow in response to God's promise: If God would give him the basics of food, clothes, and a safe return to his father's house, he would give a tenth of his earnings to God.

Jacob responded in a worthy manner to God's generous dream and revelation of himself. Let's explore further Jacob's first thought upon awakening that morning. It seems that God as author of Jacob's life began to sketch in humility.

Jacob Meets God

Rabbi Lawrence Kushner wrote a book based on a translation of Genesis 28:16, titled *God Was in This Place, and I, i Did Not Know*. He explores the musings of seven rabbis from past centuries to determine the relation of God to humankind. From this Jewish translation of verse 16 with a lower case "i" referencing Jacob, it's evident that God's encounter with Jacob caused him to immediately recognize the vast differences in Holy God and frail Jacob. The seven rabbis reveal what they learned about humility, egos, and the presence of God while meditating and arguing this verse among their peers.[1]

After he awakened, Jacob's expressed humility provides a starting point for him to discover his place in God's story. When Jacob dreamed, he deserved a nightmare. After all, he had lied. He'd abandoned his family. He'd really angered his brother. But in gorgeous mercy, God granted him a comforting, sweet dream, and because of it, Jacob would more readily recognize God's companionship as he traveled the remainder of the 450 miles to his mother's people.

How Does It Feel to Be Cheated?

Jacob arrived at his Uncle Laban's land and found that the family worked in animal husbandry. After he labored one month alongside the shepherds and shepherdesses, his uncle asked what wages he wanted. By then, Jacob had set his turban for his cousin Rachel, and he offered to work seven years to marry her. Laban agreed, and the years "seemed like only a few days to him because of his love for her" (29:20). But, on their wedding night, Laban tricked Jacob. He sent his older daughter Leah to take Rachel's place in the marriage bed. The next morning, when Jacob discovered the deception, Laban claimed that it was customary for the oldest daughter to wed first. In a week, Rachel became his second wife, but Jacob worked an additional seven years.

Jacob eventually ended up with two wives and two concubines. By the time all his children arrived, he had twelve sons and one daughter by four co-mothers. Tell me that doesn't cause household friction!

The Genesis account mentions many more hardships that Jacob encountered. His father-in-law kept changing his wages. Jacob sneaked away with his earned flock, only to be chased down by Laban. Jacob returned to his homeland but feared the first meeting with his brother. About this time, God changed Jacob's name to Israel, meaning "struggles with God."

The hardships continued. Deborah, a beloved family nursemaid, died. Rachel died giving birth to his last son Benjamin. His sons, Simeon and Levi, provoked by wrongs done to their sister, slew the males in Shechem and plundered the city. But, during all of these trials, Jacob continued making references to God's provision, his goodness to his family. At one site, he set up another altar and called it "Mighty is the God of Israel" (33:20).

- Jacob, the deceiver left his homeland.
- Jacob met God.
- Jacob received the name "Israel" (he struggles with God).

The Loss of Teen Joseph

Jacob especially loved Joseph "because he had been born to him in his old age" (37:3) and gave his favored son a richly decorated robe. And if his elaborate cloak weren't enough to arouse jealousy among his siblings, then Joseph's dream-telling was. Do you know a person who loves to share their dreams? They seem to remember what they dreamed months ago. I can't remember rolling over last night, much less my cranial-scampering that went on while I slept. But teenage Joseph remembered and told.

The setting for one dream was a grain field where his brothers' bound-sheaves of grain bowed down to his sheaf. The other dream-setting was the heavens where the sun, moon, and eleven stars bowed toward him. When Joseph recounted the one about his celestial pedestal, his family scoffed at the uppityness of the family pipsqueak.

Brotherly love long gone, his siblings soon had enough of this favored youngster, and when an opportunity came along to satisfy their thirst for payback, they sold him to a band of Midianite merchants on their way to Egypt. But the brothers held back Joseph's adorned coat, stained it with an animal's blood, and took it to their father for identification. He assumed the worse: "It is my son's robe! Some ferocious animal has devoured him. Joseph has surely been torn to pieces" (37:33).

Jacob tore his own garments, put on sackcloth, and mourned many days. His entire family came to comfort him, "but he refused to be comforted" (v. 35). The brothers remained silent and kept the deception alive for years, allowing their father to presume the worst.

I've been friends with several families who had children die at a young age. Life remolded them during that awful grief. They came out on the other side different people. For most, their new perspective brought them closer to God. A few others abandoned their faith.

When Enemy Death visits a household, as Jacob was led to believe, a somber mood envelops the grieving, as Emily Dickinson's (1830-1886) "The Bustle in a House" describes so well:

> The bustle in a house
> The morning after death
> Is solemnest of industries
> Enacted upon earth, -
> The sweeping up the heart,
> And putting love away
> We shall not want to use again
> Until eternity.

Similarly, Jacob's grief made him a different person, and that variation affected the way he made decisions about his family's future.

A New Kind of Terror

Jacob suddenly had a vacancy in his family that couldn't be filled by his other children, but he moved forward, and from all indications his faith moved forward with him, and he continued to grow closer to God. But a famine would soon come that would threaten to wipe out his entire family.

Parallel to Jacob's grief, the teen Joseph endured his own personal tragedies. A psalmist later wrote about his trials: "They bruised his feet with shackles, his neck was put in irons" (105:18). He'd gone from a pampered, pleasant life to punishment. It rained. It poured. That monsoon-trouble caused Joseph to slug through some really muddy places before he understood why he lived in Egypt.

However, throughout the biblical account of Joseph's lonely sojourn away from his family, God, in compassion, stayed by his side: "The LORD was with Joseph and he prospered . . . the LORD was with him . . . and the LORD gave him success in everything he did" (39:2-3).

God worked his good will despite sibling envy; he steadily moved Joseph to second-in-command in Egypt. He eventually married and had two sons. He adopted the Egyptian dress and language. During seven years of abundant crops, with God at hand, Joseph gathered grain enough to sustain all people and cattle within Egypt and its surrounding borders to prepare for a God-forewarned seven years of famine.

Back in Canaan, Jacob's tribe suffered from the famine, too. When Jacob heard that Egypt had grain to sell, he sent his sons, except Joseph's brother Benjamin (the youngest) to Egypt to buy grain. Upon their arrival, they met Joseph but didn't recognize him. When he inquired about their families and their father, the brothers said their youngest brother remained behind. Joseph accused them of being spies, finally sold them grain, but attached conditions: Simeon must remain behind in prison and the next time they came to buy grain, Benjamin must accompany them or they would not gain an audience with Joseph.

They returned home and recounted their adventures and misadventures to Jacob. Before long, the family ate through their grain supply, which meant they needed to return to Egypt to purchase more.

Their patriarch refused to let them take Benjamin. Jacob had reached a low point in his life: he'd already lost Joseph, and Simeon remained imprisoned. However, he had no option but to send his youngest son to the Egyptian marketplace. Relying on Almighty God, Jacob made a gallant gesture and stamped Benjamin's passport. Jacob knew possible heartache could come, but what he didn't foresee was God's unimaginable surprise.

Jacob's parting words to his sons showed his trust in God and willingness to suffer for the good of his family. He was an old gentleman, who had struggled with God, and it seemed he fully claimed God as author and finisher of his life. He trusted El Shaddai enough to "let go and let God." Jacob sent his sons off to Egypt with this blessing: "[M]ay God Almighty grant you mercy before the man so that he will let your other brother and Benjamin come back with you. As for me, if I am bereaved, I am bereaved" (43:14).

Unknown to Jacob, when he reluctantly allowed Benjamin to accompany his older brothers to Egypt, God had planned long ago to return not one, not two, but all three sons to Jacob! The scene when the eleven brothers returned home is one where I wish I could have been a fly on a camel's ear. I can picture Jacob squinting through the caravan dust to count his boys. His grin broadens as he sees eleven familiar faces bobbing among the sashaying donkeys.

I wonder who hurried to tell him, or were they all spurring their mounts and wagons onward to be the first to reach their father? With enthusiasm, his sons relayed the fantastic news: "Joseph is still alive! In fact, he is ruler of all Egypt."

Stunned by the report, Jacob didn't believe them at first. But when he saw the abundance of supplies Joseph had sent, and the wagons sent back to transport them all to Egypt, the old man's spirit revived: "I'm convinced! My son Joseph is still alive. I will go and see him before I die."

You've read the rest of this reunion story. I just want to shout, "Oh, Jacob! You get to love Joseph again, this side of eternity!" God—the giver of good gifts—will allow father and son to embrace again. Their eventual reuniting is moving. Joseph "threw his arms around his father and wept for a long time" (46:29). His old father Israel said, "Now I am ready to die, since I have seen for myself that you are still alive" (v. 30).

More Good Gifts

In no way, did Jacob ever dream that Joseph was still alive. He had only hoped for Simeon and Benjamin to return to him. We're able to read Jacob's entire story in scripture in an hour or so. But Jacob—in the middle of that live script—had no way to flip the pages to read the pleasant outcome, the story-book ending.

I found several other surprises in Jacob's story. God's goodness didn't stop in revealing that Joseph lived. Jacob's story still impacts our world. His God-given name, Israel, lives on as a prominent name among nations. And the absolute best surprise in Jacob's history resounds in our stories: "All peoples on earth will be blessed through you and your offspring" (28:14).

The Messiah arrived through Jacob by way of his son Judah. Jesus, referred to as the Lion of Judah, became the door through which each person on earth can come to the Father. And the best thing of all—Jacob's story doesn't end in our acceptance of Christ; it continues to bless on and on, generation after generation until eternity.

"God, Who Has Been My Shepherd"

In its entirety, isn't the story of Jacob beautiful? Through the brief retelling in this chapter, we see how God put meat on his deceiving, bony soul. We see that even through awful troubles, God kept pursuing, gifting, abiding, so that near the end of Israel's life, he tenderly blessed Ephraim and

Manasseh, Joseph's sons. Summoning God as their protector, he prayed, "May the God before whom my fathers Abraham and Isaac walked, the God who has been my Shepherd all my life to this day, the Angel who has delivered me from all harm—may he bless these boys" (Gen. 48:15-16).

Did you see the believing message in Jacob's prayer? He recognized God as his rear guard, his guide, and deliverer. We can shout hallelujah. We can praise. We can live content knowing that God has done and will do the same for us. God took Jacob's flimsy beginning and interlaced his goodness into his years on earth. But he didn't stop there—he went on to furnish the greatest blessing of all: God routed Jesus' arrival through that family in order to bless us.

With confidence in God's faithfulness and righteousness, we reconsider the questions posed at the beginning of this chapter. How will we now answer these?

- Can I be content with Jesus (God) as "author and perfecter" of my life and faith (Heb. 12:2)?
- Can my ego be satisfied living out the Christian cliché "let go and let God"?

Embracing Contentment
Patti Richter's Story

I walked up the driveway to our new house, a bustle of activity. My husband, Jim, directed the incoming furniture and boxes. A landscape crew worked on the yard, laying long strips of sod. Electricians finished some wiring. I stashed my purse deep into an empty kitchen cabinet so that I could get busy as well.

The house grew quiet when the movers broke for lunch and the other workers finished and left. I grabbed my purse from the cabinet to head out for some sandwiches, but it felt too light. I pulled it open and made the sickening discovery. My wallet was gone!

I frantically scanned the kitchen, and then rushed out to check my car—nothing. I drove eight miles back to our apartment, hoping I'd left the wallet there. No such luck. I felt drained and disheartened, and picked up the phone to cancel credit cards.

Halfway back to the new house, I realized I had no driver's license. Angry tears came now. Still driving, I voiced my distress to the Lord, knowing he could have prevented this trouble. "All my joy and peace in this move is gone. My whole life was in that wallet!" I raised my voice in case God didn't realize how much I'd lost.

Immediately, I sensed the Lord reply to my complaint. My lamenting stopped abruptly at the unexpected response: "I thought I was your joy and your peace. I thought your life was in me." Though inaudible, the gentle tone seemed unmistakably his.

Those soul-adjusting words quieted me. I soberly determined to get through the ordeal. But for all my efforts, I remained disappointed over the trouble that marred our move.

The first night in the new house I couldn't sleep. I recalled the lost wallet and its contents, items I'd been too rattled to think of earlier. The organizer-style wallet held weeks worth of receipts, move-related information, cash, and credit cards.

My diamond wedding ring! I had placed it in my wallet to take in for repairs. I groaned silently, remembering it and more. My sons' health records for their new schools! I'd picked up gift cards the day before. Where are those? . . . . I left them in my wallet. With each loss realized, I felt more anger toward whoever had robbed me. They're probably stealing my identity, too!

Daytime kept me occupied and distracted. But nights of tossing continued. I quit stewing about the wallet, but grew troubled over everything else, second-guessing our decision to move. Negative thoughts overtook my weary mind. How could I replace the friends I left behind? Why had we come to this big city with crime and traffic, just when Ben was learning how to drive?

As Thanksgiving approached, we looked forward to our daughter, Jayne, coming home from college, joining us in Texas for the first time. I really wanted to shake off the discontentment that shadowed me.

In prayer one morning, I confessed my bad attitude before God. But negative thoughts intruded as I remembered my stolen wallet. I'd replaced my driver license and credit cards, but many things were still missing, including my joy and peace. The selfish act of a thief had triggered this gloomy condition. Sitting there, I realized how self-defeating bitterness could be. It had been taking more from me than thieves could steal.

I asked God to bless the thief "with a better conscience if nothing else." I told the Lord I'd forgive freely if the opportunity came. I acknowledged God's perfect judgments. Things improved after that. My sleep returned to normal and enthusiasm resurfaced. Just in time for Thanksgiving.

After Thanksgiving dinner Jim explored the mechanics of our house—his first good opportunity since we'd moved in. I noticed him lying on the floor of the guest bathroom, straining to examine the plumbing under the sink. Soon he came walking toward me smiling, with something in his hand.

"I thought maybe the plumbers left a tool kit behind," he said, handing me the big, brown wallet. Except for thirty dollars, everything appeared untouched. My wedding ring, gift cards, and health records—all there! Recovering my wallet amazed me, especially knowing it could have remained hidden for years.

God's earlier goodness had already enabled me to let the matter go. The Lord knew all along where the thief hid my wallet. He could have spared me those weeks of anxiety, but then, perhaps he wanted me to find something more valuable first—that he remains the source of my joy, peace, and life.

And how appropriate—God returned my wallet over Thanksgiving weekend.

Memorize these scriptures and pray them to the author and finisher of your faith.

Praise: "How great are his signs, how mighty his wonders! His kingdom is an eternal kingdom; his dominion endures from generation to generation" (King Nebuchadnezzar, Dan. 4:3).

Petition: "LORD, I have heard of your fame; I stand in awe of your deeds, O LORD. Renew them in our day, in our time make them known; in wrath remember mercy" (Hab. 3:2).

As you consider the questions, remember:

- God helps us adapt as we wait.
- God grows our faith as we wait.
- God's answers remain superior to ours.

1. Early on, Jacob possessed a spiritual arrogance, thinking he knew best how to get what he wanted from life. Haughtiness hinders relationship with God. List two other examples of spiritual arrogance found in the Bible?

2. Deceit builds a shaky foundation to life, a place where contentment can slip away through the faulty cracks. Identify ways in which deceit affects our everyday lives.

3. After Jacob awakened from his dream, he said, "Surely the LORD is in this place and I was not aware of it" (Gen. 28:16). God can be everywhere all the time, but name a time when you especially recognized his presence as did Jacob.

4. Without implicating anyone, identify a time you were deceived. How did you react to the deception?

5. Read the account of Joseph revealing his identity to his brothers in Genesis 45:4-11. He spoke kindly assuring them that "it was to save lives that God sent me ahead of you." When someone causes us trouble, blame is an easy place to camp. How did Joseph arrive at his contentment?

6. Even though Jacob was a very old man when he arrived in Egypt, 130 years old (47:9), he adapted. How adaptable are you? How does that contribute to your contentment?

7. Jacob spent seventeen years in Egypt, but left instructions to return his body to the promised land of Canaan. What impresses you about that request? (Read Gen. 47:28-30; 48:3-4; 49:29-33; 50:1-14, Heb. 11:1; 11:13, 21).

8. Word a simple prayer thanking God for writing your name in the Book of Life, and then turn the rest of your life over to him, as author and finisher of your faith.

Chapter Nine

WAIT, ELIZABETH— GOD HAS A SURPRISE FOR YOU TOO

In the Waiting Room with God

Your prayer has been heard.

Luke 1:13

God planned that babies would take nine months to arrive in this world. Mankind thought up instant milk. God told peach trees to yield fruit once a year. Man produced fast food. God ordered the earth to rotate around the sun every twelve months. Man invented the fast lane.

How do you approach life? Do you want what you want right now? Are you waiting for a dream to come true? What sort of emotions have you experienced as you wait? How do you embrace contentment during the waiting? What if your hopes don't materialize? How will you respond if you wait a long time and don't see the desires come true in your lifetime?

"Instant gratification" defines the opposite of patient waiting. Waiting tends to be tedious, and we may not do it well. But with the holy cultivation of patience, we can receive extraordinary strength to endure long periods of waiting, much like Israel as they awaited the promised Messiah.

Through Elizabeth's story in Luke 1, let's consider her anguish over her childless state, her competent waiting, and her deliverance. Elizabeth and Zechariah spent most of their marriage years in a waiting room with God. They waited for a baby. They waited for Zechariah to serve in the temple. They waited for the Messiah.

Before Elizabeth wed Zechariah, she had the dreams of any young bride. But, I'll let her tell you all about those long years of lingering and leaning on God's mercy.

Elizabeth Tells Her Story

"I had such fun planning for the new home Zechariah and I would move into after our wedding. I daydreamed about the tasty meals I'd prepare from my vegetable and herb gardens. I even knew where I'd place each cooking pot. Yes! I even got excited over the water jars and baskets.

I also thought about the time I would soon spend alone with Zechariah. I asked Zechariah to build a low stone fence around our allotted property, so I could keep a careful eye on the toddlers God would surely bless us with.

Our wedding day finally arrived, balmy with a light mist in the air. Nearly everyone in our village attended. I'd hoped for a sunny day, but all that really mattered was marrying my beloved Zechariah.

Once settled into our new home, we often talked late into the night wondering what the future held in store for us and for our beloved nation Israel. We walked the Judean hillsides in the cool of the evening and we discreetly kissed behind the gnarly trunks of centuries-old olive trees before we hurried home.

We attended synagogue where we learned about the prophecies of our ancient fathers, and we practiced the ritual cleansings observed by the faithful in our community. Right before my wedding, I had immersed myself with an attendant at the Mikveh, a place of pure waters used for ceremonial washing. And after we married, once a month, I went to the Mikveh waters and immersed myself to obey my Lord, but to also remind me that our nation Israel had been separated from the womb of the world, that we were a holy people called apart to obey Almighty God and to usher in the Messiah. My mother had taught me the proper prayers to pray on the way to the Mikveh, prayers that call upon the love and care of the Almighty: "Guard me like the apple of your eye. Hide me in the shadow of your wings."

At the waters, I repeated other prayers while undressing completely. When I stood naked before the Lord, I vowed my total allegiance and dependence upon him as I said, "He will cover you with his pinions; you will find refuge under his wings. His fidelity is an encircling shield."

After my immersion, I affirmed where my help comes from: "I will raise my eyes to the mountain." When I arrived at my house, and before I entered to reunite with Zechariah, I repeated a lyric written by our father David: "You anoint my head with oil; my cup overflows. Surely goodness and kindness shall be my portion all the days of my life. And I shall dwell in the House of the LORD forever."

Before I rejoined Zechariah in our marriage bed and we celebrated our roles in the cycle of life, I said one last prayer asking God "to select a seed that is pure and holy so that it may tend to your work, be faithful to you, and pursue the study of Torah."

In the early months of our marriage I anticipated that I might soon stop my visits to the Mikveh when the Lord allowed me to be with child. I'd return to the Mikveh only after childbirth and my purification rites were performed by a priest. But my plans were not the plans of my Lord.

Zechariah shared my desires for a child, but, in addition, he had another dream. He longed to serve in the sanctuary of God, in the inner holy court of the temple in Jerusalem, and mingle his prayers for Israel with the incense that arose. But by this time in our nation's history, the tribe of Levi boasted so many priests that they cast lots to select those who would carry out that worship duty. We knew many who were laid to rest with their fathers and never got to burn the incense and offer prayers. Zech had regular rotations when he served in Jerusalem, and he always returned tired. Priests' work was grueling—the sacrifices, the clean up, the burning of the refuse.

Month by month, I hoped for a child, but months turned into years, and years turned into decades. Dear Zechariah and I kept all the commandments and supported each other. We wept over our childlessness and lived under a cloud of suspicion because I was barren. Gossipy women attached stigmas to any who could not have children. Some said I could not bear children because of some secret sin. Their words burned like salt in my already wounded heart.

As the years passed, so did the monthly visit to the Mikveh. By then my hair had dulled and grayed, and the arid climate caused my skin to dry, and finally all hopes vanished when my menses dried up. But I had found joy through the years in other ways. With the Mikveh visits behind me, I found relief. That season of life over, I would no longer pray—month after month—the prayers for God to bless my womb.

We finally settled in our hearts that our childless state was what it was. We had prayed for years, but the Lord had reason to withhold the blessing of children from our marriage. Instead of continually brooding or mourning our plight in life, I'd sometimes visit with our family in Nazareth, especially when Zech worked in Jerusalem. Our cousins had a sweet young daughter named Mary and she and I formed a bond, especially after her betrothal to Joseph. She plied me with questions about married life and keeping a household, and together we practiced the prayers surrounding the Mikveh ritual.

During one such visit to my Nazareth family, my hair color darkened and my skin softened. Strangest of all—my monthly cycle returned, lasted the proper amount of days and stopped. I feared an illness had overtaken me, so I returned home. After counting off the required number of days, I bathed at home, and then after dusk I made the walk to the Mikveh waters. Oh my! I cringed as I walked along with a few younger women on their way to the waters—no old women like me still visited the Mikveh to perform purification rites after her monthly cycle. I chuckled thinking, *Oh Lord, now, some will surely think 'old Elizabeth' senile.*

After my immersion, I prayed, "I will raise my eyes to the mountain." Before I entered my house I repeated the psalm that I'd said so many times with so much hope, and a fresh wound over our childlessness opened: "You anoint my head with oil; my cup overflows. Surely goodness and kindness shall be my portion all the days of my life. And I shall dwell in the House of the LORD forever."

Zechariah would return the next day, and I wept on my knees as I prayed the age old petition, "to select a seed that is pure and holy so that it may tend to your work, be faithful to you, and pursue the study of Torah."

After a restless night, I heard Zechariah enter our home before dawn. He never returned home this early, having to travel during the dangerous night hours to get here! I knew something must be wrong. I hurried to greet him, and my heart sank when the lamp light shone on his face. Although his eyes shined brightly, his wild motioning frightened me. Had he suffered a stroke in Jerusalem? He ran over to a waxed slate and frantically began to write with the pointed stylus.

He scribbled messages until my slow deciphering produced a gradual communication. The day dawned. Hunger evaded us as Zechariah continued to re-smooth the wax and write more details.

The lot had finally fallen to Zechariah to offer the holy incense in the temple. My heart swelled that his dream of serving the Lord in this way had at last come true. And, beyond that, an angel of God named Gabriel had brought a message while Zechariah ministered at the altar. No one in Israel had had a message from an angel in—we guessed—hundreds of years!

Zechariah laboriously wrote out the exact message brought to him:

Do not be afraid, Zechariah; your petition has been heard. Your wife Elizabeth will bear you a son, and you are to give him the name

135

John. He will be a joy and delight to you, and many will rejoice because of his birth, for he will be great in the sight of the Lord. He
is never to take wine or other fermented drink, and he will be filled
with the Holy Spirit even from birth. Many of the people of Israel
will he bring back to the Lord their God. And he will go on before
the Lord, in the spirit and power of Elijah, to turn the hearts of the
fathers to their children and the disobedient to the wisdom of the
righteous—to make ready a people prepared for the Lord.

I trembled as the message soaked in. I looked at Zechariah and whispered,
"Sarah. The Lord did this for Sarah."

I placed my hand on my stomach. Zechariah covered my hand. And
then he wrote the final words on the slate, "I didn't believe."

Nearly noon, and me still in my nightclothes, I finally had the story
straight. But what a story it was! We spent the day attending to our usual
chores, and several times I laughed and pushed Zechariah away when he
whispered his wishes that nightfall would hurry up. Earlier than usual,
Zech dismissed our two servants. Finally alone, we retired for the night
and I whispered with hope to the Lord, "Select a seed that is pure and holy
to attend to your work."[1]

After a few weeks, I experienced physical changes in my body, but I
happily recognized those as signs of life quickening within my womb. I
didn't want to lose this precious child I now carried, so I took it easy and
stayed in seclusion for months. I could scarcely contain my joy or news,
but I refrained from telling friends or family. Oh, you should have seen
my sweet Zechariah; his sprite walk had a bounce and skip I'd not seen
in years. Even though words now failed him, I'd see him mouthing the
psalms. I've never seen such glorious silent praise. One day his face would
alight with joy. The next day his eyes would tear up as he placed his hand
on my abdomen and felt his son John move. Our joy knew no boundaries.
Indeed, the Lord had brought us out into a spacious place.

One afternoon while resting, I wrapped my arm around my bulging midsection and reminisced about the angels' message to Zechariah: "Your prayer has been heard." Decades before when my menses stopped, I had quit praying for a child. And until my recent return to the Mikveh, I had never asked again. I pondered the idea of God storing away prayers to answer, to answer when his time was right.

Had God waited all those years to bless us with the honor of bearing the Messiah's forerunner? Did God nestle our prayers in his storehouse of blessings, awaiting his perfect timing? And the promised Messiah, would he soon make an appearance? How would I recognize him? What signs would go before him?

While pondering all of this, our servant girl walked in and announced a visitor. Before I could arise, my precious young cousin Mary rushed into the room with an enthusiastic greeting and knelt beside me. In blessing she placed both hands on my abdomen, and with a shy smile she slowly nodded affirmation as she looked into my eyes.

Suddenly, the babe in my womb leaped, and that's when I knew—I beheld the face of my Savior's mother."

The Lord May Wait to Be Gracious to You

Learning to live within God's timing may be one of the largest threats to contentment. When we pray a believing-request, we hope for an answer right then. But, just as most of us have outlived a first wristwatch, we have learned that God's timing doesn't always match our calendars. Christian humorist James Watkins says, "God is never late . . . but he sure is slow."

We so want God to understand our urgency because we need relief, rescue, or a remedy. But if God answered each prayer immediately, he would perform his mighty deeds in the framework of our wisdom and whims. Now, that's frightening. As much as I've not wanted to wait on some things, I finally understood that waiting on God is worthwhile. His timing remains superior to mine because God works within the scope of his infinite knowledge of the future, within the realm of his justice, and within the soft boundaries of his pure love. He alone knows when to answer immediately. He alone knows when to delay his response. He alone knows when to deny a request for someone's best interest.

A passage in Isaiah, originally spoken to unruly Israel, quotes God's directives about contentment: "In repentance and rest is your salvation, in quietness and trust is your strength, but you would have none of it" (30:15). I'm guilty of doing and then doing more to secure my peace. Like Israel, I'm guilty of wanting immediate deliverance from God, but remain unwilling to repent, rest, be quiet, and trust his timing. For me, that verse depicts real depth of contentment-in-waiting.

Further in that chapter, the inspired Isaiah says, "Yet the LORD longs to be gracious to you; he rises to show you compassion. For the LORD is a God of justice. Blessed are all who wait for him!" (v. 18).

If I understand that verse correctly, God longs to help, but he often waits patiently until repentance, rest, quiet, and trust begin to settle themselves in a life, a marriage, a home, a church, or a nation. He stands up. He's ready. He's eager to be gracious—to apply compassion. He knows the exact blessing to send on its way when we turn our hearts toward him. When you find yourself in a state of discontent, follow God's directives, and see that, if we will only wait, God will show up.

- Find salvation in repentance and rest.
- Find strength in quietness and trust.
- Find the Lord rising to show compassion.
- Find the Lord alongside as you wait.

Much comfort arrives through those precepts. However, I have other questions about waiting: What if I've waited for a long time? As I walk in the light of Jesus and on his path, *why* does God continue to delay his rescue . . . I need relief now.

Why Must We Wait?

Everybody waits in life. Although we have instant texting, oatmeal, and world news, some things cannot be rushed. God will not be hurried because of our impulsive wants and desires. He has and always will have our best interests in mind. But he also remains mindful of the entire earth and its inhabitants. Consider a few of the reasons we are called to live within God's timing.

- **God may choose to teach others through your life.** When a personal want, need, or dream doesn't coincide with God's plan, he may be readying you to be his visual aid. Bible prophets led tough lives as they became living-breathing-signs to wayward people. When righteous Ezekiel's wife died, his tears had to wait. God only allowed him to groan quietly; he could not weep or display any rituals of mourning (his turban remained fastened and his sandals remained on his feet). His specific grief and message signified the lonely pain God's people would soon suffer when they lost relationship with God because of their detestable practices (24:15-26). God's chosen had fallen so low beneath the plane of humanity that they sacrificed their children to godless stone and wooden idols.

- **God may choose to bring glory to himself through your waiting.** Jesus' disciples once questioned him about a man blind since birth: "Rabbi, who sinned, this man or his parents, that he was born blind?" Jesus answered, "Neither this man nor his parents sinned, but this happened so that the work of God might be displayed in his life (John 9:1-7). As part of God's plan to display his miraculous powers and affirm Jesus as the Son of God, this man suffered blindness for decades. His story has affected people for centuries, and the biblical accounting gives us one of the longest chapters involving a single miracle.

- **God may choose to perfect his power in your waiting and weakness.** Paul had a bodily ailment that he wished removed, but the apostle eventually understood God allowed the weakness "to keep me from becoming conceited" because of the intimate revelations God permitted Paul. The apostle pleaded, desperate to have this siege on his body gone. But God answered, "My grace is sufficient for you, for my power is made perfect in weakness" (2 Cor. 12:7-10). Do we allow God to do his work in our weaknesses? Even while God works through our circumstances, he also works within us, to conform us to the image of his son (Rom. 8:29).

- **God may choose the classroom of waiting to establish our obedience.** Jesus, led by the Spirit, entered a desert region where he was tempted for forty days (Luke 4:1-12). Fasting, waiting, enduring forty days of temptation, Jesus continued in obedience. The same Spirit that led him to the desert would later inspire a writer to testify: "Although he was a son, he learned obedience from what he suffered and, once made perfect, he became the source of eternal salvation for all who obey him . . ." (Heb. 5:8-9). He lived out over thirty years of patient obedience while living on the earth with sinners.

- **God may choose delays to bring more people to himself.** In the Old and New Testaments, God granted people additional time to repent and honor him, such as King Nebuchadnezzar, the citizens of Nineveh, and the prodigal son in Jesus' parable. Peter explained to early Christians who longed for the final return of Jesus: "The Lord does not delay and is not tardy or slow about what He promises, according to some people's conception of slowness, but He is long-suffering (extraordinarily patient) toward you, not desiring that any should perish, but that all should turn to repentance" (2 Pet. 3:9 AMP).

From Elizabeth's story in Luke and many other Bible stories, we under-stand that people live within God's timing of events. We also know from experience that life requires both short and long waits. But how do we wait? What will bring about contentment during our waiting? What proven steps will help us? Who lived out such an example of waiting? For answers, let's look to Elizabeth's son John, the late-in-life baby who grew into his ministry as herald for the Christ.

It's Not All about You

John's ministry and his waiting can give us specific keys to endure our waiting with both joy and contentment, especially when we remember we are part of God's unfolding plan. Consider some of the circumstances of John's life.

Zechariah and Elizabeth were told that John would be both a delight and joy to them and that he would be filled with the Holy Spirit from birth. Groomed from an early age for his ministry, the mature John recognized his role as messenger, a part of God's broad plan of salvation. He became a potent force in the region where he lived, and his ministry moved throngs of adults back to the instruction and heart of their forefathers. Many of the disobedient in John's era recognized their sins and repented.

But during John's commission, he awaited something larger than his ministry. "People went out to him from Jerusalem and all Judea and the whole region of Jordan" (Matt. 3:5). And even though his manner and message attracted thousands, John knew he waited on the cusp of some-thing larger, grander, and holier than himself. He knew he would soon fade into the background, and indeed he was willing and eager to do so.

Even though enormous crowds went out to listen to this rough-and-tumble teacher, John's trained heart searched his audiences for one person. John waited and watched for the blessed Messiah. Then finally, one day, his near kin Jesus asked to be baptized by John, and as Jesus arose from the ceremonial cleansing, a voice from heaven declared, "This is my son, whom I love, with him I am well pleased" (Matt. 3:17). Let's learn from John's waiting:

First, John recognized his role in the salvation of mankind, and he kept after the task, even while he waited for the promised Savior. Like John, we have been commissioned to introduce the Savior into the lives of our children, friends, and people we have yet to meet. Even while John waited for the public appearance and ministry of Jesus to begin, he worked toward preparing a people to receive him. John's work is our work. Through our examples, lives, and teaching, no matter what we wait upon, we'll be more contented when we remember our purpose in life—joining hands with God to prepare people to recognize and receive Jesus.

Second, John didn't turn the spotlight on himself. Even though he helped bring prostitutes and sinners back to God, he didn't gloat. Though his teaching ruffled the prayer shawls of the Pharisees, though he was anointed and appointed, he remained in the niche God created for him. His holy courage knew no bounds, and he even confronted the appointed ruler, Herod, about incest.

John recognized that the promised Messiah would be declared the Son of God. "[A]fter me will come one more powerful than I, whose sandals I am not fit to carry" (Matt. 3:11). Even after Jesus began his ministry, John reminded his disciples, "He must increase, I must decrease."

Third, when John had questions, he went to Jesus for answers. After John was thrown into prison—knowledgeable and righteous as he was—he was still human and doubts assailed him. I suspect that he thought his life might end soon, and that's why he sent his disciples to ask, "Are you the one who was to come, or should we expect someone else?" (Luke 7:19). Luke records that immediately after John's disciples asked the question, Jesus cured in their presence "many who had diseases, sicknesses and evil spirits, and gave sight to many who were blind" (Luke 7:21).

Then Jesus said to report back to John what they had seen and heard. Since John's former public messages were not accompanied by any miracles,

Jesus assisted John's belief. Jesus sent the disciples back to the prison with paraphrased words of the prophet Isaiah (61:1). John would have been very familiar with this prediction about the power of the Messiah. "The blind receive sight, the lame walk, those who have leprosy are cured, the deaf hear, the dead are raised, and the good news is preached to the poor." Jesus then pronounced a blessing over John: "Blessed is the man who does not fall away because of me" (Luke 7:22-23). To embrace God's contented peace during the stress of waiting, look to John's example. As John proved out in his life, God works miracles in hearts as we partner with our Father.

- Continue to help people recognize and receive Jesus.
- Continue to highlight God not self.
- Continue to obey even in pain.
- Continue to take doubts to Jesus.

God Reaches into Earth's Time Zones

Several years ago, I wrote a fiction story, "Wait, Elizabeth," similar to the one I shared in this chapter and *Christian Woman Magazine* published it.[2] The magazine has wide circulation in the states and elsewhere in the world and Elizabeth's story encouraged a woman-in-waiting.

Lynn and Christina had their share of waiting for a child. Eventually they had adoption paperwork completed and Christina flew to Russia to choose a child. They had asked for God's help in selecting a child to love and nourish to faith in him. When Christina arrived at the orphanage, two children were in the room. Her traveling missionary companion would adopt the little girl, and Christina asked if she could play with the little boy. No one knew if he was even available for adoption, but Christina said she immediately had confirmation in her spirit that she would take that child, Aloshia, home as her son.

Christina thought the trip would be a short one. Delays mounted. Red tape grew sticky. Empty arms ached. And, added to the stress of waiting, Christina became very ill with pneumonia—so ill that her host expected her to die.

Weak from illness and having her hopes deferred, Christina didn't think her heart could bear many more delays. Her Christian husband, parents, and siblings longed for her relief and for her return to Texas with this new son. Her church family back home continued holding her in prayer before the Lord.

One day, feeling alone and forsaken, she picked up a copy of *Christian Woman Magazine* and thumbed through the pages. An article caught her eye, especially the title, "Wait, Elizabeth." To her amazement, she saw that it was written by someone she knew. She read the story and recognized God's hand, God's timing in Elizabeth's life. She was reminded that the birth of John was part of the larger story of Jesus.

A spark of hope renewed, Christina saw her life as part of the overall story of God. A big God, who cared enough to place a magazine within her reach, a bit of hope that could stitch up her hurt and begin the healing. What she thought would be a short stay in Russia had turned into three months, but now she waited with renewed strength because God had stooped from the heavens and encouraged her. Soon, Christina had bundled Aloshia into a blanket, flown across an ocean, and settled her son in his new crib in Texas.

"Since ancient times no one has heard, no ear has perceived, no eye has seen any God besides you, who acts on behalf of those who wait for him" (Isa. 64:4).

We all have stories about waiting. For some of us, our waits are over. Others may never "see" a final outcome. Because we know that God acts on our behalf, we wait with confidence and contentment. Some of us still linger in waiting rooms, but we esteem God as faithful and righteous and so our waits become sacrifices honoring God Most High.

✺

Embracing Contentment
Leslie Wilson's Story

In early 1997, I reluctantly agreed to the purchase of a beat-up 1985 Ford F-150 pickup for purposes of hauling lumber and supplies to the home my husband, Bret, and I were building, including subcontracting and laboring ourselves. We paid $2000 cash—down from the asking price of $2250. Though the old pickup could usually make the forty-five-minute round-trip to Home Depot without adding oil, any farther than that, we didn't want to risk it.

The truck served us well for the construction of our home and the subsequent landscaping project. When we finished, Bret placed a giant sign in the windshield—Truck for Sale: $500—and parked it at the edge of our next-door-neighbor's property which fronted the highway.

A month went by without a single call.

I marked a giant black X through the $500, and wrote $300 below it.

In the following two weeks, we received only one call—from a man who offered to "take it off our hands" for nothing so he could sell it for parts in Mexico.

Again, I marked through the $300 and wrote $200 OBO (or best offer). That prompted several more phone calls like the one from the man who wanted the truck only for scrap components.

As I turned onto our street each day, I saw the truck just sitting there in the blazing sun, my scratch-through sign mocking me. Each time, I wondered why we weren't able to sell the truck. At the very least, wouldn't someone want it for an old farm vehicle?

With school starting, I didn't want to be bothered with irritating calls about the truck, so we parked it behind our house.

The second week of school, as I turned into the parking lot to pick up my daughter from kindergarten, I collided nearly head-on with an oncoming four-door sedan. Though my three-year-old son and I weren't hurt, the minivan was totaled.

After we received a nice settlement from the insurance company, Bret and I started our search for a new car we could afford. Two days later, he was laid off from his job and lost the use of his company car. Suddenly the old pickup truck ranked as the only vehicle we owned. Ah, the irony.

We scoured automobile ads for two days and found a slightly used pickup that my husband wanted to test drive. As it turned out, the same dealership had an SUV that would suit our family's needs well.

The problem? After an hour of negotiations, we were still about $2,500 apart on price. The salesman could go no lower. He'd made dozens of trips to the sales manager, whispering with him behind the tall counter while Bret and I waited in the glassed-in cubicle.

He trudged back in, shoulders slumped. "I just don't see how we can make this work," he said. "We can't go any lower. You say you can't go any higher."

I ignored the way he said the word "say."

He continued, "If only you had a vehicle to trade in . . ."

I kicked Bret's ankle. The salesman must have noticed my ever-so-slight movement because he perked up.

"Do you have a trade-in?"

"No," Bret said and kicked me back.

"We might," I chimed in. "Do you care what kind of vehicle it is?"

"No, ma'am. I don't even care if it's up on cinder blocks. We'll take just about anything—as long as you can get it here."

I spilled the details about our truck.

"Do you think you can drive it to the dealership?"

I blurted out, "Yes!" and completely ignored Bret who had rolled his eyes and shook his head.

The salesman left to go present the idea of a trade-in to his sales manager.

"Honey, this is perfect." I stroked Bret's knee. "The guy said they'd take anything—even something up on blocks. That would mean it didn't have all its wheels. At least our pickup still drives. Don't you think we can get it here?"

"I guess. I'll probably have to stop five times to put oil in it." And, for the first time since the start of the negotiations, he smiled at me.

The salesman returned, grinning broadly. "Well, it looks like we have ourselves a deal. When can you get the truck to us?"

"We'll bring it in this afternoon," Bret said. And we did—needing only one stop for oil along the way.

After we drove home our two new-to-us vehicles—Bret's truck and my SUV—we marveled at God's perfect timing. There we were, so irritated that we couldn't sell that beat-up, old pickup all summer long. God's answer to our fervent prayer at that time, "Wait on me," served only to frustrate and irritate me.

But then, he brought about the most perfect—and financially beneficial—answer of all. In his perfect timing.

Memorize and pray these scriptures as you wait upon Almighty God.

Praise: "Yes, LORD, walking in the way of your laws, we wait for you. Your name and renown are the desire of our hearts" (Isa. 26:8).

Petition: "O LORD, be gracious to us; we long for you. Be our strength every morning, our salvation in time of distress" (Isa. 33:2).

As you consider the questions, remember:

- God remains alongside as we wait.
- Elizabeth found fulfillment as she waited.
- Jesus must increase. I must decrease.

1. "And therefore the Lord [earnestly] waits [expecting, looking, and longing] to be gracious to you; and therefore He lifts Himself up, that He may have mercy on you and show loving-kindness to you. For the Lord is a God of justice. Blessed (happy, fortunate, to be envied) are all those who [earnestly] wait for Him, who expect and look and long

for Him [for His victory, His favor, His love, His peace, His joy, and His matchless, unbroken companionship]!" In this Amplified Version of Isaiah 30:18, what word(s) directly relate to contentment?

2. Read Isaiah 40:31, probably the most familiar words about strength in waiting. How are you encouraged by them?

3. Recall a time of waiting when God made you aware of his specific care for you. What stories or verses in the Bible helped you?

4. Breast cancer survivor Julie Turner shares her favorite praise about the Lord's healing and all the friends who came alongside her: "He has delivered my soul in peace from the battle that was against me: for there were many with me" (Ps. 55:18 KJV). Who has God sent to come alongside you during waiting, or a skirmish, or battle?

5. Compare this stanza of a psalm to Elizabeth's outcome: "I waited patiently for the LORD; he turned to me and heard my cry. He lifted me out of the slimy pit, out of the mud and mire; he set my feet on a rock and gave me a firm place to stand. He put a new song in my mouth, a hymn of praise to our God. Many will see and fear and put their trust in the LORD" (Ps. 40:1-3).

6. Read 1 Thessalonians 4:16-18 about encouraging each other with words about the Lord's return. Do you find contentment in thinking about the Lord's return? How often do you comfort others with thoughts about Jesus' return?

7. In the Garden of Gethsemane, Jesus waited in prayer and accepted the will of our Father. What is the difference in pleading for God to change his will or pleading for God to change your will?

8. Word a simple prayer asking for God to work his contentment within you through a current time of waiting.

Chapter Ten

STABILIZER

Trusting our Cornerstone

Let us fix our eyes on Jesus, the author and perfecter of our faith.

Hebrews 12:2

My husband and I have worked on a few building projects that call for stabilized soil where contractors mix substances into the topsoil to provide stability. From plant fibers to polymers to crushed rocks, different binders blended into the uppermost layer of earth enhance it in numerous ways—allowing it to retain water when needed, shed water, hold soil in place, or produce healthy vegetation. The soil industry offers a variety of stabilizers worked into plain old dirt which causes the soil to produce the wanted effect.

From dust, God created humankind and to dust we will return. But while living on earth, each mortal body also consists of intellect, spirit, heart, and soul. Disciples of Christ draw nutrients from Jesus-our-firm-foundation, and our bodies become living sacrifices "holy and pleasing to God," a "spiritual act of worship" (Rom. 12:1).

When faith roots deep into the Ancient of Days, contentment, joy, and peace blossom no matter what we face in our circumstances. The writer of Hebrews encouraged fixing our eyes on Jesus, who will continue to draw our faith roots deep into his living foundation. I've seen into the character of Christ through many avenues: children, friends, and scriptures, especially the Bible texts that reveal his story and his names.

Wonderful Counselor, Mighty God, Everlasting Father, Prince of Peace

One December I drove our granddaughter Natalie home after dark. Barely five, she clutched her pink New Testament in her small hands. Earlier that day, she'd played with a porcelain nativity set I display in our home through the holidays. En route, she asked if I'd like for her to tell me the story of the baby Jesus. Naturally, I said yes.

She shared the story in great detail, and I knew her parents and Sunday school teachers had done a good job of helping her understand the narrative of Jesus' birth. When she finished, she closed her Bible and said, "And he was the bestest baby of all." Followers of Christ know that his birth was only the beginning of the *bestest* story ever told.

When I study the Bible, I search out the many descriptions, teachings, actions, and names of Jesus, many of which I've shared with my grandchildren. We started with these names: Wonderful Counselor, Mighty God, Everlasting Father, and Prince of Peace (Isa. 9:6). And then I focused on teaching them the name, Immanuel, meaning God with us. But these are only a few of those revealed in holy text.

Orville J. Nave (1841-1917) compiled over two hundred names and appellations (titles) attributed to Jesus. He lists them in *Nave's Topical Bible*, and years ago I typed up that list for my personal reference. At my comfy prayer-study chair in my office, I now keep that list along with another list of over two hundred descriptive phrases about Jesus' life that I collected through my studies of the Gospels.

With a quick glance at either list, I can connect some way that my Lord stepped into my day and showed his faithfulness. That thought brings instant peace so I may acknowledge how Jesus currently abides in my life. Just last night as I went to bed, I recollected my day and a talk that I had with the mother of a special needs' child. I remembered how Jesus assists the ill—whether of mind, body, or spirit. And I pled for help in the memory of Jesus, who healed children's bodies and broken spirits.

What prompted this more intimate study of Jesus was my desire that "in Jesus' name" not become an abracadabra before the Amens. I longed for the mention of Jesus to be more meaningful than a ritual closing. I wanted to honor Jesus, remembering his intervention in my life each day. To more fully praise him for the contentment he hourly brings to my life, I continue my study of the Gospels to look at Jesus—his sayings, his interactions, and his timing when he intervened. This continuing education causes an awareness of his abiding presence.

Our living Lord remains our foundation, the source for faith, fullness, joy, and contentment.

To Compare or Not to Compare?

In our aspirations to be godly, no other person can inspire like Jesus. Susie Larsen, author and radio personality, pointed out in a blog post the dangers of comparing ourselves to others. Discontentment can glide in, take a seat, and harp away at our peace. When we compare ourselves to Jesus, we have an offer of help.

Larsen says that when we compare ourselves to another, and we conclude that we don't measure up, we may give in to defeat. However, if by comparison we deem ourselves superior, then we risk becoming conceited.[1] My best advice: Don't compare. Simply ask God to help you look like Jesus.

You may be asking, how can we "look" like Jesus? How do we embark on this journey? We can do what the early disciples did. We can follow Jesus' example as he made his teaching rounds. By reading—and rereading—the stories left for us, we can adopt his mannerisms and his compassion in working with the spiritually and physically ill. We can hear afresh the good news bound into the heart of the Son of Man. We can bask in the warmth and friendship among intimate friends. We can repeat Peter's confession, "Lord, to whom shall we go? You have the words of eternal life. We believe and know that you are the holy one from God" (John 6:68-69).

A bit of history about the traveling teachers in Israel prompts us to follow and celebrate even more our privileges in being near Jesus. Long before Jesus ever walked the earth, Jewish sages traveled from town to town teaching in synagogues, homes, and outdoors. These traveling teachers chose students who learned from their "master" so the students could in turn teach others. David Bivin says that "an itinerant rabbi was the norm rather than exception" when Jesus came into his ministry. "Rabbi," as a formal title, didn't come into use until several decades after Jesus' death. Therefore, technically, the term "master" applies more readily as a title for these teachers and for Jesus.

When a group of followers and their master entered a community, that community supported them with food and shelter. Twenty-four-hours-a-day instruction offered ample time for the students to become intimately acquainted with their teachers. Bivin notes that some one hundred years before Christ, this was a widespread saying: "Let your home be a meeting-house for the sages, and cover yourself with the dust of their feet, and drink in their words thirstily."[2] This adage from a century before Jesus supports the master and student system of the teachers in Israel, and draws a parallel to Jesus' ministry.

A similar blessing speaks to Christ-followers today: "May you be covered in the dust of your rabbi." Recalling how Jesus traversed dusty roads, presumably his followers literally had dust from his sandals fall on them, but a deeper significance would be the continual learning in Jesus' presence, as these disciples spent twenty-four-hour-days with their teacher.

The Gospels refer to numerous hosts who entertained Master Jesus and his chosen disciples—Martha and Mary, Simon the Leper, the small-in-stature Zacchaeus, and the disciple Peter. The intimacy of having Jesus in their homes during meals opened their eyes to the way of God among men, to Immanuel, God with us.

The same happens with us. Over our lifetimes, as we follow Jesus, he also becomes both host and guest in our homes and hearts. He brings the banquet. He hosts the celebration. He shows us the Father. He sends the Comforter. As such a host, he leads us in contentment. By looking at a few scenes in Jesus' time on earth, we can see how he revealed inner peace and deep contentment, and at the same time, he showed the Father to those around him.

"Mama, it's getting crowded in here."

How do you feel about crowds? I'm an extrovert, so I enjoy small gatherings or larger crowds, but whenever people outnumber the square footage of the building—that's too crowded even for me. At the Houston Livestock Show and Rodeo, our family of four and one guest walked in an exhibit hall looking at displays. Our visit coincided with thousands of others, and after thirty minutes we could barely move. Our daughter mentioned the over-crowding and then her friend said, "Wasn't there an outbreak of measles in Houston?" Just the mention of such a virus had us gasping for ventilation. My 6'4" husband spied an "Exit" sign and led the way outdoors.

Once Jesus' ministry began and he healed that first person, the weary, expectant crowds soon followed. Massive. Constant. They kept him from sleeping, from eating, from teaching his disciples. They forced him to cut short the mourning of the death of his cousin, John the Baptist.

Obviously Jesus didn't have enochlophobia, a fear of crowds. Rather, he had a heart for their plights. Let's "fix our eyes" on Jesus in the midst of a crowd and consider his demeanor and examine his self-control and compassion.

Learning to Live in the Name of Jesus

Recently, I wrote a short study for my home church on the book of Mark. As I did so, I was reminded of how many times the word "immediately" appears in the text. Jesus knew busy. Jesus understood a crowded schedule, and Jesus dealt with literal crowds. I'm convinced Jesus experienced far more urgency in his days than we do. The word "immediately" appears forty-two times in the book of Mark.

Jesus dealt not only with the physical crowds, but his days presented a steady stream of needy people who pressed him for attention. Let's look at Matthew's account (15:29-39) of Jesus providing food for four thousand people to discover how he remained contented and kept his servant spirit toward the multitude for three days.

Matthew says that Jesus' location was hilly, and that people brought those who were unable to get to him on their own. Can you picture that? Aged mothers and dads struggle to lead their blind and lame adult children around small boulders. Can you feel the sorrow yet see the hope as a young couple carries their fevered child to Jesus? Can you imagine single persons with no one to help them, their knees growing raw as they pull their lifeless legs along?

Mingled among that crowd were the curious, the chronically ill, the political, the hecklers, and the dying who simply wanted more of life. Even those weighted by wrong-living gravitated to this hill to hear more of his teaching. After the healings and restorations, people stayed with this teacher—the only one with miraculous powers. The men alone numbered four thousand, and their stay lasted three days.

Let's think about the second night of those three days in that outdoor area. The crowds probably slept on cloaks on grassy patches or propped against rocks. That evening many little campfires burned, babies cried, and dogs barked, accompanied by a litany of scritchy sounds—the mix of crickets, frogs, and nocturnal bugs singing out as they were meant to do.

During the night, as Jesus lay listening to the sounds of four thousand plus people—shifting, rolling over, and snoring—did their presence bother him? Did he rub his arm that had gone to sleep and think, "They're all still out there"?

Four thousand men on a hill conjures up a village, not a picnic. When Jesus lay down, the clustered crowd pressed in from every side; when he woke up, they remained all around him. When Jesus stretched and rubbed the sleep from his eyes on that third morning, the thousands of men, women, and children milled around, waiting to hear from this teacher and watch him perform miracles.

I imagine Jesus greeted God, his station in life, and the people with a smile.

Because he didn't view these people as interruptions but opportunities. He saw them as the messengers of tomorrow. He knew some of them would eventually carry his message to others.

How does Jesus' three days on just this one occasion compare to my days? I've had long to-do lists, but I've never awakened to over four thousand people waiting for me to rise and shine for the third day in a row! To do that, one must be content in life, with full acknowledgement of one's role as servant.

At least two conclusions emerge about Jesus' love and care for the four thousand. First, Jesus handled with ease the crowds, which contained both the thrill-seeker and the sincere-seeker, because he knew his purpose in life. He knew his support system—his Father. He was in business with him—a Father and Son business—the people business.

Jesus didn't get flustered by the many, many people on that third morning. He continued to teach, serve, and provide food with a side dish of genuine love. The same Jesus ably assists today's followers who awaken to continuous back-breaking tasks. For months, even years, some lovingly assist a family member who has Alzheimer's disease or cares for a special needs' child. Another may serve a prison sentence to pay off debts to society. Jesus knows what it's like to wake up and be greeted by the same monotonous—and possibly heart-wrenching—scene every morning.

He can and will give grace-filled interaction and endurance. His joy continues to ignite smiles in his servants. Jesus invested his time in people.

He focused on caring for people. Today, many things clamor for our attention. We get so trapped in the small details of everyday life that we often don't remember the big screen, the screen God sees, the overall picture of the earth and God's redeeming work.

But when our eyes are fixed on Jesus, we remember the cloth from which we are cut. We are clothed with Christ. He continually forms himself in us. We can be wise in the way we act toward outsiders because Jesus was wise in the way he acted toward people. We can make the most of every opportunity because Jesus made the most of every opportunity. Our conversations can be full of grace and seasoned with salt because Jesus' conversations were full of grace. And, we can grow to the point that we know how to answer everyone because Jesus knew the perfect answer to every situation (Col. 4:5-6).

Second, Jesus knew when to retreat. When we make time for Jesus, his peace embraces us. His contentment forms a calmness of spirit within us, and we know when to retreat from our "crowd." On this occasion, Jesus gave for three solid days—teaching, nurturing, healing, praying, and feeding. Then he sent the crowd away and retreated to refuel.

On the days when many people come my way, I pray in the name of Jesus who awoke to four thousand needy people. I ask God to make me as generous as Jesus and to give me the discernment to know when to back away and say, "Go home."

As we abide in Jesus, his peace awakens and grows within us. When we can greet each day in his name, when we can live the middle-of-the-day in his name, when we can say goodnight in his name, that's when his contentment and everlasting joy has moved in to stay. "And whatever you do, whether in word or deed, do it all in the name of the Lord Jesus, giving thanks to God the Father through him" (Col. 3:17).

- Be wise in the way you act toward outsiders.
- Make the most of every opportunity.

- Season speech with grace.
- Live every minute in the name of Jesus.

Let's look at one more scene, when Jesus was twelve and his parents lost sight of him as they traveled from Jerusalem back to Nazareth.

Losing Sight of Jesus

As a mother, I've wondered how Joseph and Mary lost sight of Jesus. His parents probably assumed that at the age of twelve, he could look after himself in the company of foot-traveling family and friends (Luke 2:41-52). Other distractions may have existed for Joseph and Mary by then. It's possible that they had quite a few more children on that journey. Since Jesus' age was twelve, Mary could have borne several more children by then. Jesus could have had up to five siblings from ten to newborn by this time.

Just picture it. Six kids . . . a road trip . . . a walking road trip at that . . . and one donkey. I'd love to probe Mary's feelings and know how she really felt when she imagined she'd misplaced God's Messiah. After contemplating this story, I better understand Joseph and Mary losing sight of Jesus, especially after comparing how often I'm distracted and lose sight of Jesus in my daily life.

I fully understand how his parents assumed he was with their family. By the time they'd gone a day's journey, and then walked back to Jerusalem, and finally began their search, three days had passed—likely with increasing degrees of worry.

That's what happens in my life too. When I lose sight of Jesus, assumptions rule my life, not grace and truth. When I lose sight of Jesus, worries multiply. When I lose sight of Jesus, I live in frenzied days until I fix my eyes upon him once more.

Near the end of Jesus' life, he knew the disciples would not be able to see him much longer, and said, "In a little while you will see me no more, and then after a little while you will see me" (John 16:16). Although Jesus had revealed the marvelous plan of the Comforter arriving, he also understood the heartache of losing someone's physical presence.

The disciples questioned among themselves about his apparent riddle—seeing him, not seeing him, and then seeing him again. Jesus explained that they were about to go through a time of grief, but like a woman in childbirth has pain and then joy after her baby is born, so would be their future. When the old law gave way to a grace-filled new covenant with Jesus as executor, their joy would be complete.

Jesus assured them that joy was coming and help was on the way: "I tell you the truth, my Father will give you whatever you ask in my name" (vv. 22-24). He further encouraged them to exercise this privilege of asking the Father in his name: "Ask and you will receive, and your joy will be complete" (v. 24).

Though Jesus' remarks on the night before his crucifixion were directed to his disciples, we can expect similar results when we:

- Keep Jesus in sight.
- Ask in his name.
- Expect Jesus' promised joy and peace.

Jesus didn't want his beloved disciples to lose sight of the fact that they had a firm foundation in him, even though his physical presence would no longer bless them. Their faith roots could extend deep into the Ancient of Days through Jesus' name. Their partnership with the Father, Son, and Spirit would produce contentment and joy in their lives and would multiply the gospel-task-force. We honor these men who remained faithful to the end. For when furious storms battered their topside, they held fast to their stabilizer, Jesus Christ their cornerstone.

✠Ⓢ〜

Embracing Contentment
Bradley Q. Owens' Story

I grew up knowing God loves me. I've grown as a person, a Christian, a writer, and a minister honored to proclaim God's love on the page and in the pulpit, and I've long known deep contentment as near as my next breath.

Maybe that's why I was so surprised by the tsunami of discontent that swept over me some years ago, the swells of which still sometimes threaten.

When my family and I moved to a small community to serve a little church, I hoped to stay for more than a few years—never expecting to stay more than twenty-five. But I have.

Largely blue-collar with a solid group of core members from that wonderful World War II generation whose every cell is colored with the DNA for long-term loyalty, the little church had a reputation for exceptional love and a passion for Christian unity.

Those things matter to me. They mattered to our leaders. And, in many ways, those things did not change. But something did.

What changed? Only a slight shift in the leadership. Some leaders who had been unfailingly supportive and warmly relationship-oriented died or moved. We added one or two "successful" leaders more familiar with a business than a family model. I began to feel the quality of support I'd always enjoyed slipping a bit. I found myself feeling more like an employee being managed and less like a well-loved and respected minister.

I found myself surprised by the overwhelming force of discontent that swept over me. I was disappointed in our leaders. I felt hurt and, I admit, angry. Even though most of them would still go through the fire for me if push came to shove (a situation you never want in a church), they were too meek to stand against more dominant personalities.

Almost drowning in waves of unhappiness, I felt like a wimp as I dealt with a situation that for many of my colleagues has been the unhappy norm. I began to question my decision to stay. Did the "marriage" matter only to me? Was it not the precious thing I'd thought it was, worth giving the best years of my life and ministry to nurture? I'd always felt God's blessing on the church, the relationship, and my decision to stay. In addition, I felt deeply disappointed in myself. My morose mulling over the situation had cost time and productivity.

I wish I could tell you I've conquered the storm and can testify with the apostle Paul, "I've learned to be content whatever the circumstances." Though the situation has improved in some ways, I'm still sometimes caught by surprise at the strength of breaking waves of discontent. But when I feel my contentment in danger of being washed away yet again, I employ a few coping mechanisms I've learned.

I've learned to pray for God's strength and comfort—not in the kind of agonized lengthy prayer that actually focuses me more on the problem but simply in oft-repeated short heartfelt prayers for God's healing and power.

I've learned that getting out among God's people and engaging in real pastoral care and ministry, sharing their lives and joys and struggles, chases away black clouds of depression that gather when I focus on me.

I'm learning to focus more on supporters whose love, friendship, and respect are more real and substantial than the criticism of a few.

I'm learning that thanksgiving will warm my heart.

I'm learning more about God's blessing of Sabbath. Perhaps not a particular day, but regular times—short or more lengthy—when I pause to simply be and not do. To read. To rest. To play. I need that.

Most of all, I'm learning that God remains faithful. He teaches me through difficulty what I can never learn in comfort. I'm learning that contentment from God can be found, *must* be found, even in the storm. I even suspect that if I will be patient, God will change some of the circumstances I've described.

I've a wry suspicion that my Father will do that right about the time I, his child, learn the secret of trusting and being content with the circumstances just as they are right now.

Memorize and pray these scriptures as you build your life upon the Lord Jesus Christ.

Praise: "The Lord is my rock, my fortress and my deliverer; my God is my rock, in whom I take refuge, my shield and the horn of my salvation" (2 Sam. 22:2-3).

Petition: "Restore to me the joy of your salvation and grant me a willing spirit to sustain me" (Ps. 51:12).

As you consider the questions, remember:

- Fix your eyes on Jesus.
- Recall his many titles.
- Recall his ministry among people.
- Ask in his name.
- Live in his name.

1. Write down five favorite names of Jesus, the ones that reveal God-attributes that minister to you.

2. What's your favorite story about Jesus? Why? Describe the characteristics you see in Jesus in that story.

3. "Do not think of yourself more highly than you ought, but rather think of yourself with sober judgment, in accordance with the measure of faith God has given you" (Rom. 12:3). Christian faith and bestowed gifts grow at different speeds. What from this verse relieves you from comparing yourself with others?

4. Read Matthew 7:24-29, and then recall a literal thunderstorm with high winds and imminent danger. Did you feel secure in your location, or did you wish for better founded shelter? To what did Jesus compare the hearing and practice of his words? What do the high winds, rising streams, and torrential rains represent?

5. Will you make the same proclamation as a teacher of the law who came to Jesus, "Teacher, I will follow you wherever you go"? (Matt. 8:19).

6. Recall a time when you gave all your mind and body could give, and you knew it was time to retreat and seek refreshment of body, mind, and soul. During rest, in what ways do you seek comfort from God?

7. Choose a name or description of Jesus from the following list and write why that name speaks contentment to you: Lord of Hosts; the Beginning and the End; Son of Man; Branch; Bread; Shepherd; Unspeakable Gift; Wonderful Counselor; Prince of Peace; Jesus, who noticed dusty feet; Jesus, the Sabbath healer.

8. Write a three sentence prayer stating your confidence and adoration to Jesus, your Savior, and ask for the same contentment he received from his Father.

Chapter Eleven

NOURISH YOUR THOUGHT LIFE

The Feeding and Care of the Soul

Do not conform any longer to the pattern of this world,
but be transformed by the renewing of your mind.

Romans 12:2

I'm *not* as nice as I think I am.

I imagine that more of the world's ways creep into my life than I realize. Recently, I worked at my dad's house with my adult daughter. After returning to my home, my daughter, Sheryle, said to me, "Mom, I thought you were a bit short with Grandpa." Her observation startled me, because I thought I spoke in cordial tones to my dad.

Still bothered, I later said to my husband, David, "Sheryle said that I spoke in a sharp tone to Dad today."

His gentle reply: "You probably did."

I was crushed to think that an unkind attitude had slipped into the conversation that I'd had with my senior dad, who is dealing with a decade of my mother's illness and years of her confinement to bed.

But that's the nature of sin. It sneaks in and grows and develops briars, unless we allow God's sweet, contented Spirit to feed us and eradicate sin-thorns.

We live on a small Texas cattle farm, not in a manicured subdivision. We constantly battle our acreage, mowing pastures and managing the wild Cherokee rose. If left unchecked, the rose bushes can grow thorn-ridged vines, thick as a thumb. These can form hedges reaching twice the height of a very tall man and fifteen-feet deep. Let them get out of hand and it can cost hundreds of man hours and thousands of dollars to restore the land.

Every thorn on earth represents this word from God, who said to Adam, "Cursed is the ground because of you; through painful toil you will eat of it all the days of your life. It will produce thorns and thistles for you, and you will eat the plants of the field" (Gen. 3:17-18).

Pristine neighborhoods may only have the thorns of cultivated roses. With supermarket food available, suburbanites rarely labor in the sun battling thistles to put food on their tables, but I think every urban family should own at least a potted thorn bush! Thorns remind us that sin can take over a life, if the Holy Spirit of God isn't allowed to fill our vessel, if he isn't allowed to dwell fully within to spade the heart-soil and turn up roots of subtle sins.

Any sin left undisturbed can grow thick impenetrable hedges around hearts and halt the growth of God's blessing of contentment. Once, when I taught a class about subtle sins, a woman we lovingly tagged Ma Bo, still malleable in her nineties, confessed to committing some of the subtle sins. Her confession gave me such hope, and pointed to God's promise that someone stronger than ourselves stops sin in our lives and nourishes good growth at any age.

Fruit of the Spirit

I recognize God's holy patent on love, joy, peace, patience, kindness, goodness, faithfulness, gentleness, and self-control (Gal. 5:22). At one time I viewed the fruit of the Spirit as a list of accomplishments to seek and increase in my life. However, after striving for years to realize more Spirit-fruit in my life, I found they are not a to-do list. I cannot create them in my life. The fruit of the Spirit increases in my life when I daily yield to the reign of God in my heart.

The fruit of the Holy Spirit allows us to recognize subtle sins, confess them, and ask for God's merciful forgiveness, allowing us to embrace more holiness each time we yield to his indwelling. The Amy Foundation's list of about fifty subtle sins helped me to watch for those sins which can gnaw holes into my soul. Here's a sampling from the list: inflexibility, laziness, closed-mindedness, dogmatism, egoism, lack of affection, resentment, insincerity, guilt, bitterness, gluttony, and prejudice.[1]

Let's consider three of God's innate qualities—listed as fruit of the Spirit—and how, through them, he uproots and crowds out sin. As God tills our hearts with love, self-control, and joy, he replants his goodness. The more of God we accept and welcome, the more his contentment abides within us.

"God Is Love"

People love chocolate and chocolate labs. We love mini poodles and mini bagels. We love movies and movie popcorn. We say the word "love" in many casual ways. God put genuine love in motion when "he gave his one and only Son, that whoever believes in him shall not perish but have eternal life" (John 3:16). A chasm of charity exists between our general definition of love and God's character of genuine love. God shows his love toward us in thousands of intricate ways. The most remarkable to me remains that he still allows any of us, with our penchant for going our own way, to keep breathing the air he created. But as Graham Cooke said, "He is not disillusioned with you—He never had any illusions about you to begin with."[2]

Most of us comprehend God-kind-of-love, but if asked to describe it using concrete words, we find that more difficult. With such thoughts in mind, one day I paid attention to the cows resting in the pasture underneath the shade of a huge live oak. I said aloud, "Lord, that's it." It took that scene for me to come to a deeper realization about God-love: "When we can nap safely in someone's shade, that's love."

We word-sling love around as if its usage carries no obligation. John said, "Dear children, let us not love with words or tongue, but with actions and in truth" (1 John 3:18). Paul told us what love looks like when he wrote to the Corinthians—that love is patient, kind, and that it doesn't envy or boast. Also, love is not proud, rude, self-seeking, or easily angered. In Paul's description of divine love, here's my personal favorite in his list of attributes: "love keeps no record of wrongs." I bask in God's forgetfulness of my sins!

But Paul doesn't stop there in his description. He couples the word "love" with that absolute word "always": love always protects, always trusts, always hopes, always perseveres (1 Cor. 13:1-13). Our relationship with God has full-measure love that tills out sins and contents us with new growth in him.

Notice the similarities in the description of the love-actions in the Corinthian passage and the fruit of the Spirit in Galatians. God the Father, God the Son, and God the Spirit continually share all those inherent qualities with us. Adopted as a child of God, we inherited his Spirit, who teaches us how to live out love.

Some of the most beautiful passages in biblical poetry describe God's love as shade or shelter. When nominee-for-Israel's-throne David fled from his enemies and sought refuge in a cave, he called to God to have mercy on him, saying, "I will take refuge in the shadow of your wings until the disaster has passed" (Ps. 57:1). Another psalm says that "the LORD is your shade at your right hand" (Ps. 121:5).

Watching our small herd of cows seek shade-shelter gave me an additional description of love. Shade represents protection, safety, rest, and times of refreshing. As God-disciples we also provide shady rest for family and friends. We simply come alongside someone with a blessing because God's generous Spirit fed us and we, in turn, give to others. When we witness the wilting of friends, we know they must have shade to survive. They need refreshment away from pressures, and that's when we cast a goodly shadow over them.

And so I ask, who among your family and friends join God in shading your life? Who provides shelter from blistering, energy-draining circumstances? Who rallies around you when you can no longer help yourself? With certainty, I can tell you it's not inanimate things that we often say we "love"—chocolate, bagels, or popcorn. No. Real people provide our shade, the ones dedicated to love-lived-out, a Spirit trait.

God has the ultimate loving wingspread, and he instills in his children the desire to come to the aid of others. For authentic contentment, give thanks for the Almighty's sin-weeding, protection, and love-increases in your life. Give thanks for your companions, who also provide God's shelter.

Come, Lord Jesus, and ladle out a generous helping of your love.

- Whom will you shade?
- Who will shade you?

Self-Control

When things go our way, we proceed through a day in relative calm. Why not? Life's good. No one crosses, insults, or toys with our emotions. But when spouses, children, coworkers, or even strangers rub us the wrong way, we can get irritated and respond in less than a godly manner. Christians who have acquired Spirit-fueled "self control" have both power and skills from the Holy Spirit to limit their thoughts, actions, and reactions.

Yielding to the Holy Spirit, we gain self-control which continues to oppose mean-spirited spewings and actions. Merciful God grants followers a say-so over bad habits, and we no longer have to rely on human-spirit willpower to overcome sins that threaten to get us off track.

Here's an example of an aggravation that could cause an out-of-control spirit: As I walked through a bank door, I noticed an older man right behind me, so I held the door open for him. He marched past me and stood at the front of the line waiting for the tellers. I stood back in wonder.

The teller asked, "Who's next?" He never looked back and moved up to the counter. Right then, I had a choice to make—to stew over having to wait or to ask a blessing on his day. I reasoned (with God's nudging), how could I possibly know what was going on in his life to cause him to neglect common courtesy? I didn't know anything about him, so I excused him and backed it up with a prayer for his day.

I'm not telling you that to pat myself on the back. I'm telling you that to give God's Holy Spirit a great big pat on the back. Blessing and praying for someone causing me a lengthy wait doesn't come naturally to me. I used to fume. Maybe tell someone else about his lack of manners. Bemoan the delay. And the incident might have spoiled—because I allowed it to—half of my day.

You've had hundreds of similar incidents of rudeness—intended or unintended—happen to you, too. Minor irritants can work us up into a small squall. You've seen how those dirt devils pop up on the landscape. They twirl in a dither, pick up bits of debris, and sling them everywhere.

Of course when everything goes our way, it's easy not to get ruffled. But when trouble crimps the day—even then—that's when we can ably control our thoughts, actions, and reactions because of God's indwelling and urging.

Come, Lord Jesus. We're hungry for gigantic portions of your self-control.

- Yield to the Spirit of God, who gives self-control.
- Practice self-control, which blesses others.

Joy

Our two-year-old granddaughter Molly loves to be outdoors, and she wanted to go outside one day when we kept her. However, the heat index had reached 104 degrees, and I officially melt at that level. "Not today, Molly. It's too hot."

She didn't kick or scream when I told her. But, disappointed, she lay facedown on the cool pine floor remaining silent and sad for a few minutes. Then, up she came—off to play again—in her usual happy mood.

One winter, Jolie, our five-year-old granddaughter, went to school several days when gray skies ruled and outdoor temps ranged in the teens in South Texas. On the weekend, a sunny day finally came along, but the outdoor temps remained in the low twenties. Jolie's mom looked up just in time to see Jolie walking out of their home. Clad in a two-piece bathing suit, sun glasses, and with a rolled beach towel under her arm, she was ready for fun in the sun. Young children don't comprehend the seasons—they simply trust their eyes to tell them if it's sunny outside.

As little ones grow up, they learn that they can't trust their indoor-sight to reveal the outdoor temperature. Understanding the seasonal changes does that. Similarly, Christians have received a permanent joy that has nothing to do with the "temperature" surrounding us. We can successfully embrace an abiding joy, peace, and contentment beyond the world's comprehension.

God's gift of joy does not depend upon sunny weather or circumstances. We can be in the throes of grief and still retain the joy of God. It may not bubble to the surface on our faces at those times, but his joy remains rooted within us.

Having joy as a permanent gift enables us to "enjoy" and "rejoice." The prefix "en" means "in" or "into," an act of taking in pleasure. We can enjoy numerous things—from meditation on deeper things of life to the sight of a majestic mountain.

Also, the gift of joy gives us the ability to rejoice. The prefix "re" can mean once or repeatedly. We get to experience joy through one-time events—at a baptism or a wedding. Or, we rejoice again and again each time we see our loved ones or spouses or a sunrise. Bible reading can produce rejoicing, as we comprehend the multi-layers of God's goodness. Smiles spring from the depths of joy. Take the hand of a young child and walk into any retirement home to see how seasoned-with-life faces light up to see someone so freshly molded from the hand of God.

A prophet wrote about how God, again and again, finds us enjoyable: "He will take great delight in you, he will quiet you with his love, he will rejoice over you with singing" (Zeph. 3:17). The word "rejoice" means that God repeatedly delights, quiets, and sings over us. Can anything you touch, feel, or experience compare to that?

Sherwood E. Wirt's *Jesus, Man of Joy* digs deep into the character of God and how divine joy was displayed in the life of Jesus. If you pursue a study of "joy" through the Bible, it will change your life. My oldest Bible was bought thirty years ago, and I marked passages that say "joy" or any modification of that word with a stick figure, hands lifted high and a smile on his face.

People too often see God as a stern figure ready to smack down any dissenter. Wirt identifies the problem with that notion: "God did not create the human race to become its Judge; rather He created it to become its Father." And, "[w]hat the Bible says about wrath and judgment is not based on God's doings at all, but on God's reactions to our doings."[3]

According to www.BibleGateway.com the words "joy," "rejoice," and "enjoy" or other variants appear over five hundred times in the NIV Bible. Why such emphasis on joy? I'm no theologian, but I've learned that when Jesus restores what was lost, rejoicing is the natural response of heaven. Luke records three "joy" stories that Jesus told about a "found" sheep, coin, and son (chapter 15). The words of the parable-father whose son returned indicate a spontaneous expression of joy depicting God's joy: "[W]e had to celebrate and be glad" (v. 32).

In stressing Jesus' superiority to the angels, the Hebrew writer quoted Psalm 45:6-7, tagging Jesus with more joy than any other being. "You have loved righteousness and hated wickedness; therefore God, your God, has set you above your companions by anointing you with the oil of joy" (Heb. 1:9).

We don't achieve this joy. God's joy remains a gift connected to the salvation of our souls. We can receive in increasing measure the intrinsic joy experienced between the Father, Son, and Spirit. They bought and brought us back from our captor. And they bring us back to themselves, the great source of joy.

With pure abiding joy, Paul could address problems and know joy at the same time. He admonished two women, Euodia and Syntyche, to get their act together. Well, actually, he said, "to agree with each other in the Lord," and then in his next few pen strokes he wrote celebratory words to the whole church in Phillipi: "Rejoice in the Lord always. I will say it again: Rejoice!" (4:2-4).

Although no one is exempt from difficulties that require our thought time and steady prayers, through Paul, God encouraged us to vacation our thoughts on: "whatever is true, whatever is noble, whatever is right, whatever is pure, whatever is lovely, whatever is admirable—if anything is excellent or praiseworthy—think about such things" (Phil. 4:8).

By spending time with God in his Word, in solitude, in good thoughts, and in prayer, he can give us more of the joy that reverberates in the heavens. There's a party going on in the Bible. Have you noticed?

Come, Lord Jesus. Sustain us with the "good news of great joy."

- Grow our joy, one day at a time.
- Make us ambassadors of joy.

Awaken My Ear to Hear the Word of the Lord

"Here I am! I stand at the door and knock. If anyone hears my voice and opens the door, I will go in and eat with him, and he with me" (Rev. 3:20). At one of my blogs, I have a captioned picture of a little girl with unruly hair pouring a cup of tea, and the scripture beneath says, "I will come in and sup with him and he with me."[4] Is anything more beautiful than that? The Lord announces his presence and longing for connection with enthusiasm! Are we listening? Are we always open for a spoon-feeding from God?

When Solomon inherited the king's throne, God gave him opportunity to ask for "whatever you want me to give you." If God asked me that, I'm afraid I'd have to ask for a sabbatical to think about it. It seems Solomon praised the Lord and then asked, "Give me wisdom and knowledge, that I may lead this people, for who is able to govern this great people of yours?" (2 Chron. 1:7-12). Solomon asked for a listening ear to lead with God's assistance.

Isaiah told how the Lord awakened his ear each morning, and how Isaiah made a habit of listening. Old Testament scholars believe that same text describes the relationship of Jesus with the Father—that God-in-heaven and Jesus-on-earth communicated around the clock, "uninterruptedly."[5]

> The Sovereign LORD has given me an instructed tongue.
> to know the word that sustains the weary.
> He wakens me morning by morning,
> wakens my ear to listen like one being taught.
> The Sovereign LORD has opened my ears,
> and I have not been rebellious. (Isa. 50:4-5)

Indeed Jesus would verify that he said or did nothing of himself (John 8:28). Through Isaiah we receive a keen glimpse of the constant communication between Father and Son. Therein lies our challenge, to fully receive the communiqué of God. And when we do that, he will daily feed us.

This age offers so many diverse ways to hear the Word of the Lord. Through electronic gadgets, we can literally pull the Word of God out of thin air (through radio waves, a form of light God spoke into existence). When God commanded eons ago, "Let there be light," who knew that meant we could choose to receive Bible words through that light source.

Our body needs food and water for nourishment; no one would dispute that. Our inner person needs nourishment, too. Most would agree with that. But far too many have made a practice of feeding the body while starving their souls. What if we reversed that order? What if we cut down on what we actually take in as nourishment, and upped the quantity of God's word, solitude, meditation, quietness, and worship.

The world offers junk food—the ingredient list is scary. But just think how we could promote Christ, if we took the unhealthy world-feedings off our menus? Think of the good that comes to us and through us when we feed at the mercy table.

The love-filled, self-controlled, and joy-filled Savior summons:

- "Come follow me."
- "Come unto me."
- "If anyone thirsts, let him come to me and drink."
- "Behold, I stand at the door and knock."

We can't add to God's glory, but we can become flashing neon signs or gentle whispers that spread his fragrance. A song I rejoice in and sing along with speaks of the availability of the Godhead and proclaims we are "Trinity blessed." Let those words sink into your soul—Trinity-fed day after day, if we only answer the door. To receive that around-the-clock nurture from God and his abiding contentment, awaken each morning and repeat the compelling words of the lad Samuel, "Speak, for your servant is listening" (1 Sam. 3:10).

Embracing Contentment
Charlotte Maluski's Story

Empty-nesters at last, my husband and I were all set to travel and enjoy life. Our daughter had married and our sons would soon head back to college. Contentment reigned.

Until the phone rang at 2:30 a.m. jarring me from a sound sleep. I fumbled in the darkness to locate the cordless phone on my nightstand. When I finally picked up the receiver, the caller asked for my husband. My husband talked quietly for a few minutes and hung up. He then turned to me, "Charlotte, Robert's dead."

My whole world screeched to a halt when I heard that my beautiful twenty-one-year-old son had been killed in a car wreck. I wanted to roll up into a tiny ball, hugging my knees to my chest. I wished I could turn back time or rescue Robert or trade places with him. The physical reaction—heaving sobs and gasping breaths—helped me spew my disbelief, but my mind and heart couldn't process such a tragedy. This couldn't have happened! He had been in our home just hours before. Part of my heart departed that night. An emptiness settled into my soul that will never completely be filled until I am reunited with my precious son.

I recalled that Robert had lovingly assured me that if I ever needed to get hold of him, all I had to do was call and he would be there. Now he and his promise were gone.

Robert was the youngest of our five sons—the one who made little league baseball, boy scouts, and junior high band concerts seem new and full of fun, even though it was our fifth go-'round. Then, just like that, he was gone from our lives.

One of my other sons heard the phone ring that night and came to check on us. After we told him about Robert, he asked to pray for us. I remember only one line of his prayer: "God, thank you for twenty-one years with Robert."

As if on autopilot, we moved through the days before and after the funeral. I clung to the poignant words in my son's prayer. I kept reminding myself that not everyone is fortunate enough to have a "Robert" in their lives. I should be grateful for the precious time I enjoyed with this wonderful young man of God. Our family and children gained strength and comfort and support from one another and from friends. Then, as usually happens, friends and family resumed their own lives in the following weeks.

Each member of our immediate family dealt with the loss in his own way. My husband and I mourned Robert on different grief-paths. I felt numb, stricken, lost. I didn't know how to make it through this terrible time. Early on, I resolved not to ask God why Robert died. But nagging doubts crept in. I fudged on my own rules, coming up with other "whys." Why did Robert die so young? Why couldn't God have taken me instead? Of course, I was still questioning God, but in my grief-stricken mind, I fooled myself into thinking I wasn't.

In sadness, I often nestled into a comfortable chair in my bedroom—the cushy sides curved around me, cocooning me, making me feel safe. Sitting in that chair, I prayed Psalm 23 again and again.

Hours would pass as I closed my eyes and visualized a setting where I lay under a spreading tree in a green meadow filled with beautiful wild flowers. Other times, I imagined myself sitting beside the clear, blue waters of a running stream. I felt the physical presence of Jesus there, as though he stood behind my chair with his arms around my shoulders. That chair became our meeting place, and he accompanied me on my journey through loss. Together, we walked through the "valley of the shadow of death." And even amidst the shadows, I could see Robert running—as he loved to do—in eternal fields. I began to understand that Robert now abided happily in the "house of the Lord, forever."

During this time, my faith expanded, deepening as never before. The presence of Jesus was very real. Although my "Why?" question had never been answered, I found a hook to hang it on: That would be the first question I would ask at "St. Peter's gate." When I shared that notion with my husband, he told me—with a grin—to be very good so I'd be sure to get there someday.

Months went by, and a curious surprise blossomed slowly. I began to experience a sense of contentment. That doesn't mean I stopped grieving—not by any measure—because my broken heart ached terribly. As long as I breathe, a part of me will always wish that Robert had lived to experience the rest of our family's journey. But a peaceful acceptance settled in my soul. I understood that whatever reason God had for Robert's death at such a young age, it had been a part of his plan.

Even in my sorrow, God supplied me with contentment and trust in his goodness.

Memorize and pray these scriptures expecting God to nourish your soul.

Praise: "Blessed is the man you choose and bring near to live in your courts! We are filled with the good things of your house, of your holy temple" (Ps. 65:4).

Petition: "Sir, give me this water so I won't get thirsty" (John 4:15).

As you consider the questions, remember:

- Allow God to feed your soul.
- Allow God to weed subtle sins.
- Allow God to reproduce Spirit-fruit.
- Allow God to open your ears.

1. "Do not conform any longer to the pattern of this world, but be transformed by the renewing of your mind" (Rom. 12:2). What efforts do you make to disconnect from the world and connect with God for mind renewal?

2. Examine this statement: If we go to the dark side in our thoughts or actions, we always take someone with us. How have you experienced this to be true or false?

3. Even human fathers know how to give good gifts to their children. Jesus said our Father will give the Holy Spirit to those who ask (Luke 11:11-13)? Do you practice this? How often do you make this request part of your prayer life?

4. The Lord says, "Open your mouth wide, and I will fill it" (Ps. 81:10). Verse 11 gives two keys to opening our mouths—listening and submitting? What spiritual feeding do you receive from God when you listen and submit? How have you realized contentment when you listen and submit?

5. "Blessed are those who hunger and thirst for righteousness" (Matt. 5:6). Is this your mindset? In your everyday walk, what do you crave the most?

6. Compare Jacob's hip-wrench (Gen. 32:22-32) to Paul's "thorn in the flesh" (2 Cor. 12:7-10). Think about these men's constant physical ailments. Yet, God's power was perfected in weakness. Have you seen such divine work in your life?

7. When Jesus revealed himself as the "Bread of Life" (John 6:25-59), a crowd responded, "Sir, from now on give us this bread" (v. 34). Yet Jesus mentioned their unbelief in him. What's the difference in wanting what Jesus can give and wanting Jesus?

8. Word a simple prayer, asking for more of the Holy Spirit, more of the Bread of Heaven, and more of the holiness of God Most High.

Chapter Twelve

ONE MORE LAP AROUND MOUNT SINAI

Relearning life-lessons

Aim for perfection. . . .

2 Corinthians 13:11

The cactus suspended overhead caught my attention, and I stopped to look at the unusual sight. Walking through Lady Bird Johnson Park in Fredericksburg, Texas, I spied a prickly pear cactus rooted into the damaged limb of a live oak.

My curiosity aroused, I contacted Hap Hollibaugh from Cactus Jungle in Berkeley, California and inquired about the cactus "bed." He said most likely this prickly pear was "simply an advantageous grower." Hollibaugh further said plant seeds sometimes germinate in odd places if they find enough nutrients, and a single prickly pear pad could hitchhike to branches "by sticking to a bird."[1]

The spiny plant, fifteen feet off the ground, was tagged an "advantageous grower" because it used available provisions. When squeezed into unyielding circumstances, the tiny plant aimed at doing what it was created for despite abnormal conditions. The cactus in that oak tree created a visual of blooming where planted.

My dear friend, Jan Tickner, commented that we spend a good deal of time in life re-learning old lessons. Because we experience uprooting and replanting many times, life may call on us to be an advantageous grower in new environments. That's what Jan calls making "one more lap around Mount Sinai." In this final chapter on contentment, we'll make a last lap. And in our jog around, we'll look at commitments which increase the child of God's contentment—devotion to giving, devotion to gratitude, and devotion to worship.

Devotion to Giving

When I see the stooped backs of older gentlemen, I'm sometimes moved to tears. I realize what their bent frames represent—years of labor to support their families. When I see the knotted hands of aging women, I know what those weakened hands symbolize—years of work and service to family and friends. Lives poured out, living sacrifices spent in service to others.

Paul mentions his work for money to support himself and his companions and in that context repeats the words of Christ, "It is more blessed to give than to receive" (Acts 20:35). But as we all know, all giving does not involve money. But I will venture to say that all giving involves mercy—mercy toward someone who has a need.

Such giving occurs in many ways, but especially through individuals, churches, and charitable organizations. This past year I became acquainted with Rachel Eggum Cinader, the founder of Dress a Girl Around the World. Her organization works in conjunction with her brother's non-profits, Hope 4 Kids International and Hope 4 Women International. Established nearly four decades ago, the parent organization supplies medical and dental needs, village wells, and opportunities for international trips where Christians assist with hands-on help in villages.

After I found out about Rachel's specific goal of giving girls the dignity of owning at least one dress, I wrote a newspaper column about the project and the "pillowcase dresses" they make and deliver. Several of my readers, from youth to seniors, contacted me to say that they and a group of friends had joined together to make pillowcase dresses. A group of students and their sponsor from The Woodlands College Park High School made garments and sent them to Dress a Girl. Newspaper column reader and avid volunteer, Nicki Wright also emailed, "Two weeks ago two friends and I finished twenty-one pillow case dresses and last week we mailed them to Hope 4 Women International and their Dress a Girl Around the World program .... We have about thirty more pillow cases and will work to get them done."

From Rachel I learned that the giving of the dresses sometimes coincides with a village's celebration of their new water well. She said the dresses are not handed out en masse among these remote villages in Uganda, but that she or a volunteer present the dresses individually. We "kneel in front of them and make the moment special—we look into their eyes and tell them that Jesus loves them."[2] Can you picture it? Fresh water. Fresh faces. Splashed with living water.

Those meetings between giver and receiver remind me of the Samaritan woman who met Jesus at the well (John 4), and then returned to her village and invited others to meet him. When we practice Jesus-type-giving, at least a two-fold blessing results: The receiver is blessed and the giver receives joy and contentment from God. Other benefits spring from such giving, too. As we obey and seek the good of others, joy multiplies in our lives—just another way for Jesus to shine his light through us.

The contented-in-Jesus person will find no shortage of ways to give—on the home front and internationally.

- Jesus, urge us on to continue your blessing of giving.
- Jesus, thank you for refreshing your givers.

Devotion to Gratitude

When I think of giving thanks to Almighty God, I'm reminded of a small drama that played out in front of me at a grocery checkout counter. Slender, tiny, about five, and dressed in light blue overalls and T-shirt, he could have been an extra in Andy Griffin's Mayberry. The boy waited in a grocery store line to purchase a package of toy cars. Eyeglasses perched atop the bridge of his nose.

When his turn came, the female teen clerk scanned the barcode and announced the amount of $6.48. Solemn faced, he reached into his overall bib pocket. Out came a child-size zippered wallet. With great care, he took out one dollar at a time, laid each bill down and counted. "One . . . two . . . three . . . four . . . five."

In his depleted wallet, I caught the flash of coins. He needed at least a dollar more. Silent, I mouthed to the clerk that I'd cover it, and passed a dollar over his head. She asked him for "Forty-eight cents." He could count dollars, but coinage counting baffled him. His pennies didn't add up to his need.

I passed another dollar above his head to cover the difference. Sale closed out, her cash register spit out fifty-two cents change. Silver coins slid down a chute into a metal receptacle. He heard the coins hastening his way, peeked into the silver bowl, scooped up the change and zipped it in his wallet.

The clerk looked at me. Quiet, I whispered, "Let him have it." By then, I'd have paid ten dollars to watch the scene play out all over again. He was that cute. He walked toward a woman in another check out line, probably his grandmother, to show her the purchase he'd made *all by himself*.

But nothing in life is done *all by oneself*. When Paul engaged the Athenians in conversation about their objects of worship, he zeroed in on their generic altar dedicated "TO AN UNKNOWN GOD" (Acts 17:23). These cautious worshipers, not wanting to offend any god, had paid homage to all.

After Paul introduced those Greek philosophers to God, with their own poets' words he explained, "For in him, we live and move and have our very being" (Acts 17:28). Every eye twitch, every flexed muscle, every breath, powered by God. No cell, DNA, soul, or goings-on exist without him. Darryl Tippens in *Pilgrim Heart* says, "All of life is the proper arena for divine activity."[3]

When Mayberry boy showed his purchase to his grandmother, his joy surfaced. Purchase accomplished. Job completed. Goal fulfilled. But at the moment of his rescue, he wasn't aware of a larger, unseen supply-hand that passed above his head.

The apostle Paul tells the Athenians that God made the entire human race from scratch and made the earth "hospitable, with plenty of time and space for living so we could seek after God, and not just grope around in the dark but actually *find* him." He further says, "He doesn't play hide-and-seek with us. He's not remote; he's *near*. We live and move in him, can't get away from him!" (*The Message*).

On days when we need extra energy, time, talent, money, or mercy to make it through until lay-me-down-to sleep time, God bends near; he's forever shifting blessings our way from his unseen world. How many times has he walked ahead of us and cleared a path in traffic or relationships or business dealings so we're not caught in destruction? Only God knows.

On the flip side of God's nearness, seeing, and doing for us, we can give thanks that God overlooks us all the time. (Yes! That's what I meant to write.) Think about it. When he looks at those who are clothed with Christ, he doesn't see our individual frailties. He keeps no record of wrongs. Tears fall as I write that. He sees our needs. He hears our pleas, but when he sees us he looks through the Holy One Jesus—our betrothed—who stood in for us and paid the penalty for our sins.

Author Leigh McLeroy asks, "What if we viewed our lives as one long, tender engagement—as a prelude to a promised eternity with a strong and faithful Bridegroom?"[4] What if that reality became our mindset?

I remember my engagement as a time of thanksgiving—full of joy, contentment, and excitement about the future. I showed off my engagement diamond ring. I told anyone who would listen about our wedding plans, and I recounted numerous reasons why I loved David— his commitment to God and belief in the fidelity of marriage, his work ethics, his wit, and his adoration of me. What if every day we realized our time on earth as a betrothal to Christ and lived that out in thanksgiving?

As the Orthodox Jewish male wakes each morning, and before he ever stirs, he recognizes that he opens his eyes because God ordained him to live another day. With each physical act of getting himself ready for the day, the worshiper recites a corresponding blessing toward God. Among the many morning traditions he adheres to, one especially caught my attention, the recitation from Hosea, where God informed Israel that they would call him "my husband." In thanksgiving, today's Orthodox Jewish male, each morning, repeats God's vows to Israel:[5]

> I will betroth you to me forever;
> I will betroth you in righteousness and justice,
> in love and compassion.
> I will betroth you in faithfulness,
> and you will acknowledge me as LORD. (Hos. 2:19)

If you are like me, even though I long to constantly give thanks to God, I often forget to give praise. We can aim for putting God in first place each day; we can reprise our role as bride and recall that we're getting ready for the happiest wedding ever.

- Holy Spirit, teach us bride-purity.
- Holy Spirit, teach us the contentment of minute-by-minute gratitude.

Devotion to Worship

Too often, we connect acts of worship to a church building. Meeting with others to worship remains a highlight of my week, but so do the times I sit alone in my home communing with God. Worship can also take place when I drive and pray and sing along to worship songs. Or when I break out in prayer when cooking, folding clothes, or writing. Or when I hold my husband's hand or give a hug to a wheelchair-bound nursing home patient. Or when a Muslim clerk asks me if I'm a Christian because I don't give in to his sales pitch to buy a lottery ticket. And then he says, "I'm fascinated by this Jesus of yours." And I get to tell him a little more about "this Jesus" of mine.

As the Holy Spirit has allowed me to grow in Christ, I now spend some of my life in the deeper end of the pool remembering that all of our experiences can be worshipful, but too many of them remain separated in the shallow end. But I have experienced enough joy in the depths to find that all of life—its moments, its length—can become worship.

The singing group, Revival, recorded a song titled "Worship with Your Life." When Christians adopt that biblical and healthy mindset of twenty-four-hour service to God, our worship becomes continual.

I remain in awe of the courage of the prophetess and early-widowed Anna of Luke 2 fame. When I was younger, I often wondered after reading the brief verses which describe her entire life of service, "How could she spend all those years living so simply in the Temple?" She fasted and prayed night and day until in her mid-eighties. Since I'm older-in-the-Lord, I've changed my mind and the question. I now ask, "How could she not?" She accepted an opportunity of lifelong worship and God honored her by allowing her to witness within the temple when Immanuel, God came near.

She obviously experienced an unfathomable relationship with God because of her life devoted to worship. She remained constant in prayer and fasting. And, when Joseph and Mary presented the Christ Child at the temple and offered sacrifices for Mary's purification, Simeon, another devout worshiper, took baby Jesus in his arms and prophesied about him. Anna approached them and gave thanks for the child and told everyone about him.

We, too, can become twenty-four-hour-a-day worshipers because our temples house the Holy Spirit. The popular hymn, "Here I Am to Worship," written by Tim Hughes has become a favorite of mine. So much so that when I enter my kitchen to clean, cook, or serve others, I sometimes sing the lyrics because I see my work as worship, laying down my life to the Lord to comfort my family, to ready them to serve the Lord in their individual capacities. At that particular moment, my life is a living sacrifice, my kitchen the particular altar where I serve.

According to the *Encarta World English Dictionary,* "worship" means "adoration, devotion, and respect"[6] given to deity. That definition is the first listed usage of the noun "worship." I like that definition best. Other usages of the word "worship" connect it to a place such as a synagogue, church building, or place of prayer. But as Jesus said to the Samaritan woman, "Yet a time is coming and has now come when the true worshipers will worship the Father in spirit and truth, for they are the kind of worshipers the Father seeks" (John 4:23).

When we begin to see all of life as worship, not just scheduled events, we can begin to anticipate the holiness of God in our workplace, at lunch with a friend, at Little League practice, or at the crib changing a diaper. Worship cannot—and should not—be isolated to a specific time or place. The next time you face a task—pleasant or unpleasant—try singing the lyrics to "Worship with Your Life" or "Here I Am to Worship."

The Final Lap

Sometimes when my faith slumps over, I recognize my downcast emotions and ask myself a question. Perhaps you would like to answer it, too: What part of "surely goodness and mercy shall follow me all the days of my life" do I not understand? God prepared a table in the desert for millions of people for forty years, furnishing food and water and clothing and shoes that didn't wear out. And besides meeting their physical needs, he led them to a gradual understanding of his holiness and an unbridled love that wanted relationship with them. Trusting his care, we can live as advantageous growers and keep learning contentment as we make laps around our oasis and deserts.

Jesus told a story about a man who sought bread from his friend "because a friend of mine on a journey has come to me" (Luke 11:5-8). When we embrace God and his contentment, the warm light of Jesus becomes evident to others. When friends on their journeys pass through our lives, we can guide them to the bread of life, Jesus the Savior of the world.

After Jesus told that story about one persistent friend asking another friend for bread—at midnight, rapping on his door, requesting three loaves—he summed up his message with these poignant words: "Ask and it will be given to you; seek and you will find; knock and the door will be opened to you. For everyone who asks receives; he who seeks finds; and to him who knocks, the door will be opened" (Luke 11:9-10).

God placed his people who had learned obedience in the desert at the crossroads of the ancient trade routes, a land where he would eventually introduce himself more fully through Jesus, the Christ. As we embrace God's gift of contentment, our lives will intersect other lives many times. It remains our privilege through all our days to lead those journeyers to the Prince of Peace.

- Ask for contentment; receive contentment.
- Seek contentment; find contentment.
- Knock. The door to contentment will be opened.

The LORD bless you and keep you;
The LORD make his face shine upon you
and be gracious to you;
the LORD turn his face toward you
and give you peace. (Num. 6: 24-26)

Embracing Contentment
Barbara Warren's Story

My parents worked hard to provide for us, and though I can't remember going without anything I really needed, I still wanted many things. We simply couldn't afford them. As the years passed, I continued yearning for things just beyond my reach. Many times, I wasn't even sure what I wanted; I just had a nagging sense of not being completely satisfied.

The popular girls in school seemed so sure of themselves, sporting their new, store-bought clothing. Meanwhile, my shy and introverted self wore home-made dresses or hand-me-downs. I couldn't help but compare myself to them. Though I wasn't jealous of what they had, I just wanted more.

After I grew up and married Charles, my husband and I always had a fairly nice place to live. We didn't drive new cars, but neither did our friends. We managed to pay our bills and have a little money left over, but something seemed to be missing. I wanted more.

During our relocation to the city, Charles and I dreamed of moving back home to the country. Eventually, we bought a farm and became livestock producers. Instead of going to a job every day, I worked at home, raising a garden and canning and freezing the produce. I loved the farm and enjoyed our life there, but again, it wasn't enough. I wanted more.

I bought and read magazines filled with pictures of beautiful houses and decorating tips. I lived in an old farmhouse, and no amount of decorating advice could turn it into an elegant show place. My house boasted a cornfield on the left and a cow pasture on the right. In truth, I liked my comfortable home, but as I flipped through those magazines, I yearned for what I couldn't have. I wanted more.

Some time later, I attended a writer's conference and left with a determination to start a writer's group. I contacted several others who had expressed an interest and we met together. None of us were really sure what we were doing, but we resolved to do it anyway. To my surprise, I had moderate success with my writing, but my dreams of producing a bestseller and getting rich eluded me. As usual, instead of being satisfied with what I had, I wanted more.

One of the women in our writing group had been a missionary in Mexico with her husband. One night she told of a man who invited them to his home. It turned out to be a very dilapidated shack with a dirt floor. When it rained hard the family had to pile their belongings on top of tables because water would run under the walls and get everything wet. The man wanted to have prayer with them before they left. She said she broke out in goosebumps when she heard him pray, "Father, thank you for my house."

Her words cut through me. Suddenly, I saw myself in a new light, and I didn't like the person I saw. I thought of all I had, all the many ways God had blessed me, and I felt ashamed. I had overlooked all the treasures I had already been given in my endless quest for more.

It rained that night. Thunder and lightning split the sky while I lay in a warm bed, sheltered from the storm. Humbly I whispered, "Father, thank you for my house."

Of course I didn't change completely overnight, but I'm aware of the need to live a life of thankfulness, to find joy in giving and be less consumed by getting. Then, I ran across Proverbs 30:7-9, a scripture passage I felt God had written just for me: "Two things I ask of you, O LORD; do not refuse me before I die: Keep falsehood and lies far from me; give me neither poverty nor riches, but give me only my daily bread."

God knows what is sufficient for me, and life is more fulfilling when I put my needs and my wants in his hands and let him sort it out. I'm now learning to be content with what I have. And when the old feelings of discontentment taunt me, I count the ways he has blessed me, and I whisper, "Thank you, Father, for all you've done for me. Thank you for my house."

Memorize the following prayers to help you stay on pace to perfection.

Praise: "Hallelujah! For our Lord God Almighty reigns. Let us rejoice and be glad and give him glory! For the wedding of the Lamb has come, and his bride has made herself ready. Fine linen, bright and clean, was given her to wear" (Rev. 19:6-8).

Petition: "O righteous God, who searches minds and hearts, bring to an end the violence of the wicked and make the righteous secure" (Ps. 7:9).

As you consider the questions, remember:

- Aim for perfection.
- Be devoted to giving.
- Be devoted to giving thanks.
- Be devoted to worship.

1. *Contentment learned from our trustworthy God brings satisfaction of mind and heart in feast or famine.* As you've journeyed through this study, have you embraced more contentment? How?

2. Jesus said, "It is more blessed to give than to receive" (Acts 20:35). Describe a time when you experienced the truth of Jesus' statement.

3. What scripture or thought in this study has stuck with you and most encouraged you to keep learning contentment?

4. Jesus told a parable about the sheep and the goats (Matt. 25:31-46). The righteous—who fed the hungry, gave drink to the thirsty, clothed the naked, and visited those in prison—seem to have no concept of basic theology that what was done for others was done for Jesus. Why do you think they are called righteous even though they didn't have a lot of knowledge?

5. In what ways do you personally "worship with your life"?

6. The early Christians met together every day, ate together, and praised God. Read Acts 2:42-47. What other things did the early disciples do? How did the community accept them? Who did the Lord add to their fellowship?

7. "Therefore, there is now no condemnation for those who are in Christ Jesus, because through Christ Jesus the law of the Spirit of life set me free from the law of sin and death" (Rom. 8:1). Even though imperfect, we aim for the perfection of Jesus Christ. How do the words of Romans 8:1 impact your contentment?

8. Word a simple prayer praising God and asking our generous Father to fill your life with his contentment so that through you, God's peaceable light will shine.

NOTES

Chapter 2: Cliff Dwelling

1. David Wolpe, *World's most humble man*. Retrieved from http://www.sinaitemple. org/learning_with_the_rabbis/writings/The%20. Used by permission.
2. Retrieved (2009, June 17) from http://www.hymntime.com/tch/bio/c/r/o/ crosby_fj.htm.
3. Retrieved (2009, June 17) from http://en.wikipedia.org/wiki/Fanny_Crosby.

Chapter 4: Worrisome Ways

1. *Pulpit Commentary*. 1962 ed. 16, *Mark & Luke*. H. D. M. Spence and Joseph S. Exell (Grand Rapids, Mich.: Eerdmans, 1950), 285.
2. Ibid.
3. *The Transforming Word: One-Volume Commentary on the Bible*, Mark W. Hamilton, ed. (Abilene, Tex.: Abilene Christian University Press, 2009), 804.

Chapter 5: Permit Loads

1. "The National Center on Addiction and Substance Abuse (CASA) at Columbia University." http://www.casacolumbia.org/templates/ChairmanStatements. aspx?articleid=581&zoneid=31, (accessed May 2009).

Chapter 6: Bedazzled

1. Chip MacGregor, "The Writer's View Yahoo Group." http://groups.yahoo.com/ group/TheWritersView/, (accessed May 2010). Used by permission.
2. John Naish, *Enough: Breaking Free from the World of More* (Hodder & Stoughton, 2008).
3. John Huxley, "Sydney Morning Herald," February 7, 2009, http://www.smh.com. au/news/national/and-now-for-the-good-news/2009/02/06/1233423495139. html, (accessed June 2010).
4. Cyndy Salzmann, "America's Clutter Coach." http://www.cyndysalzmann.com/, (accessed April 2010).
5. Elise Boulding, "Elise Boulding Quotes." http://thinkexist.com/quotes/elise_ boulding/, (accessed June 2010).
6. http://www.freecycle.org/, (accessed June 2010).
7. Mindy Starnes Clark, *The House That Cleans Itself* (Eugene, Ore.: Harvest House Publishers, 2007), 99. Used by permission.

Chapter 7: Living from Scan to Scan

1. Beverly Grayson, "John's Wife." http://www.johns-wife.blogspot.com/, (accessed October 2009). Quotes from blog posts used by permission.
2. Cathy Messecar, *The Stained Glass Pickup: Glimpses of God's Uncommon Wisdom* (Abilene, Tex.: Leafwood Publishers, 2006), 109.
3. David Bivin, *New Light on the Difficult Words of Jesus: Insights from His Jewish Context* (Holland, Mich.: En-Gedi Resource Center, 2005), 139.
4. Tim Hansel, "Notable Quotes: Christian Living." http://apprehendinggrace.com/ category/quoted_people/tim-hansel/, (accessed June 2010).

Chapter 8: Jacob, God Has a Surprise for You

1. Lawrence Kushner. *God Was in This Place & I, i Did Not Know* (Woodstock, Vt.: Jewish Lights Publishing, 2000).

Chapter 9: Wait, Elizabeth—God Has a Surprise for You Too.

1. Rabbi Nina Beth Cardin. *Out of the Depths I Call to You: A Book of Prayers for the Married Jewish Woman* (Northvale, N. J.: Jason Aronson, Inc., 1992), 38-54.

2. Cathy Messecar, "Wait, Elizabeth," *Christian Woman Magazine*, September/October (1995), 12-13; 61-62.

Chapter 10: Stabilizer

1. Susie Larson, "Deeper Life in Christ. Powerful Life on Earth." http://susielarsonblog.typepad.com/, (accessed June 2007).

2. David Bivin, *New Light on the Difficult Words of Jesus: Insights from His Jewish Context* (Holland, Mich.: En-Gedi Resource Center, 2005), 10-12.

Chapter 11: Nourish Your Thought Life

1. "Church Writing Group Lesson Plans. Lesson Six: Dealing with Subtle Sin in our Lives." http://www.amyfound.org/writing_resources/church_writing_groups/lesson_plans/lessons/lesson_6.html (accessed August 2010).

2. Graham Cooke, "December's Newsletter Article." http://grahamcooke.com/index.php?fuseaction=e4_news.display_full&news_id=67&e4=enqiooialgdrqaa4ell5sb7fq5, (accessed July 2010).

3. Sherwood E. Wirt, *Jesus Man of Joy* (Eugene, Ore.: Harvest House Publishers, 1999), 72.

4. Cathy Messecar, "The Stained Glass Pickup." http://stainedglasspickup.blogspot.com/.

5. *Pulpit Commentary.* 1962 ed. 10, *Isaiah.* H. D. M. Spence and Joseph S. Exell (Grand Rapids, Mich.: Eerdmans, 1950), 248.

Chapter 12: One More Lap Around Mount Sinai

1. Hap Hollibaugh, www.cactusjungle.com (accessed 2005).

2. "Hope 4 Kids International." http://www.hope4kidsinternational.org/dressing-girls-at-the-wells, (accessed August 2010).

3. Darryl Tippens, *Pilgrim Heart: The Way of Jesus in Everyday Life* (Abilene, Tex.: Leafwood Publishers, 2006), 15.

4. Leigh McLeroy, "Wednesday Words Newsletter." (accessed 2009).

5. Milton Steinberg, *Basic Judaism* (New York: Harcourt Brace Jovanovich, 1975), 122-123.

6. *Encarta ® World English Dictionary © & (P).* Microsoft Corporation, 1998-2004.